MURDER RAP

THE UNTOLD STORY OF THE BIGGIE & SMALLS TUPAC SHAKUR MURDER INVESTIGATIONS

GREG KADING

Some names have been changed to protect the privacy of certain individuals connected to this story

Published in the United States by One-Time Publishing LLC

Library of Congress Cataloging-in-Publication Data

Kading, Greg.
Murder Rap: The Untold Story of the Biggie Smalls and Tupac Shakur Murder Investigations/Greg Kading.

ISBN 978-0-9839554-8-1

Printed in the United States of America on acid-free paper

www.MurderRap.com

First Edition October 2011

To Afeni Shakur and Voletta Wallace

Whenever human justice fails,
rest assured that God's prevails

CONTENTS

PART
ONE

"Hit 'Em Up"

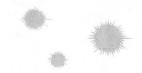

THE MIRACLE MILE is one of the most famous and familiar addresses in Los Angeles. An imposing strip of high rises, museums and landmark buildings, it runs down Wilshire Boulevard straight from the heart of Beverly Hills. Along the broad six-lane thoroughfare, the cream of L.A. society—movie stars and sports figures, politicians and tycoons—come to see and be seen, in an endless round of gallery openings, charity events and nightclub photo ops.

The Petersen Automotive Museum is a late but prestigious addition to the Miracle Mile, and one of the city's premier venues for high profile partying. Located on the southeast corner of Wilshire Boulevard and Fairfax Avenue, its parking structure running another block down Fairfax, the Petersen's stylized tail fin facade faces directly across the street from the Art Deco-style May Company department store, the gold-plated new addition to the Los Angeles County Museum of Art. Together the two guard the western gateway of the renowned boulevard, and it's hard to imagine a more prime piece of real estate than that occupied by the four-story, 300,000-square-foot showcase of automotive history.

The museum, opened in 1994, features five rotating galleries spotlighting a priceless array of vintage cars, a state-of-the-art showcase for auto design and technology, and a glass-walled penthouse conference center. But it is the second floor of the museum, the Grand Salon, that makes the Petersen ideally suited to the kind of celebrity-studded events for which the Miracle Mile is best known. The polished onyx floor, auto-inspired décor, and displays of one-of-a-kind luxury and concept cars are the perfect setting for galas, receptions, and black-tie functions. From almost the moment it opened its doors, the Petersen was the setting of choice for L.A.'s most prestigious social occasions.

The evening of March 9, 1997, was one such occasion. The night before, at the downtown Shrine Auditorium, the Eleventh Annual Soul Train Music Awards had spotlighted a new generation of black music superstars. Although the show's hosts included the sixties R&B great Gladys Knight, and the program included a Heritage Award to the legendary soul singer Curtis Mayfield, it was clear to everyone in the house that the torch was being passed.

And among the more significant new torch bearers was a 6'3", 360-pound Brooklyn-born rapper named Christopher George Latore Wallace, aka Biggie Smalls (after a character in the 1975 film *Let's Do It Again*), aka Frank White (the hero of the 1990 film *King of New York*), aka the Notorious B.I.G., or aka, simply, Biggie.

Although he had not been nominated in any category, there was no doubt that Biggie Smalls represented the future of music. His second album, a double-disc set titled *Life After Death*, was two weeks away from its highly anticipated release and already the intentionally leaked track "Hypnotize" was a huge radio hit. It was easy to hear why. With a hook based on a sample from the Herb Alpert instrumental "Rise," the song was a perfect showcase for Biggie's trademark loose and easy flow and his compelling, autobiographical rhymes. Within days of its official release "Hypnotize" would rocket to number one.

Biggie had been invited to the awards to present the trophy for Best Female Vocalist. Sharing the podium with him that night was Sean "Puffy" Combs, riding high with his own chart-topping single, and recording debut, "Can't Nobody Hold Me Down." Combs, a multitasking musical entrepreneur, was a major player on the exploding rap scene. With his own string of aliases, including Puff Daddy and P. Diddy, Combs was most commonly known simply as Puff for his childhood habit of "huffing and puffing" when he got angry. The Harlem native, son of a murdered drug dealer, Combs began his meteoritic ascent as a concert promoter before breaking through with his own label, Bad Boy Records, in 1993. The company's first signing: Biggie Smalls.

Combs had since gone on to oversee every aspect of Biggie's career, co-writing and co-producing "Hypnotize" along with the subsequent *Life After Death* hits, "Sky's The Limit" and "Mo Money Mo Problems," tracks that owed much of their success to Combs' flair for polished production. Combs would, in fact, go on to almost singlehandedly bring rap music into the mainstream, helping create the smooth, listener-friendly genre of commercial hip-hop, the most successful form of popular music since rock and roll.

But in the Shrine Auditorium that night it was hard to imagine that the gangster lifestyle celebrated in the music of Biggie Smalls could, by any stretch, be considered in conventional pop terms. What Biggie and Puff were formulating in the studio and on stage would redefine what constituted socially acceptable entertainment. It was raw, profane, and unapologetically in-your-face.

Its polarizing effect was underlined by the fact that not everyone in the audience that night greeted Biggie and Puff with ecstatic cheers. As they stood to present the award to Toni Braxton, scattered jeers and shouts of "West Side!" could be heard ringing out under the hall's high ceilings.

"What up, Cali?" Biggie murmured, leaning into the microphone. But the booing only got louder as the tension rippled across the auditorium. West Coast gang signs were flashed in the glare of the TV lights. It was obvious that the Notorious B.I.G. and his mentor, Puff Daddy, were in hostile territory.

Biggie had, in fact, been camping on the enemy's doorstep off and on for four months prior to the award show. He had wrapped up the recording of *Life After Death* in a Los Angeles studio and gone on to shoot the video for "Hypnotize," a $700,000 outlaw-on-the-run fantasy co-starring Puffy Combs, using locations in downtown L.A. and Marina Del Rey.

Accompanying him everywhere was his large posse, including members of a rap group made up of assorted friends from his Brooklyn neighborhood, known as the Junior M.A.F.I.A. (Junior Masters At Finding Intelligent Attitudes.) Their 1995 debut album, *Conspiracy,* was produced by Biggie and featured the platinum-selling hits "Player's Anthem" and "Get Money," on which he is featured. Among those who had escorted Biggie to the West Coast was his cousin, Junior M.A.F.I.A. member James Lloyd, aka "Lil' Caesar," and Damien Butler, aka "D-Roc," who was constantly at Biggie's side.

The entourage had checked into the Four Seasons Hotel, where they stayed for two weeks before being thrown out after an altercation between the rap star and his then-girlfriend Tiffany Lane. They had bounced in and out of various hotels over the next several days, finally ending up at the plush Westwood Marquee just prior to the Soul Train Awards.

From the moment he had set foot in Los Angeles, Biggie was also surrounded by a phalanx of professional bodyguards. Puffy Combs had hired Ken Story, owner of the Los Angeles-based T.N.T. Protection Service, for round-the-clock security, beginning with Biggie's arrival at the airport. Also on duty was Paul Offord, head of security for Bad Boy Records, and Reggie Blaylock, a moonlighting Inglewood police officer, retained by Story to provide additional muscle. As a result, there was never fewer than a half dozen heavyweights following the rapper and his crew wherever they went. "We take precautions," Combs told *MTV News* in answer to a question about his retaining the services of an off-duty cop. "The people that defend this city, we hire them to protect and defend us."

Combs had good reasons for insuring protection and defense. As rap music's popularity began to take hold in the early nineties, its promoters and producers went to great lengths to downplay the controversial rivalry between the music's West Coast and East Coast contingents. It was nothing more than a publicity stunt, they insisted, designed to sell more records by creating competition and letting fans choose sides.

The facts, as clearly heard in the music itself, suggested otherwise. Rap's legitimacy as an authentic expression of street life and the gang-banging ethos could hardly be overstated. Given that credibility, it was hardly surprising that rap artists garnered intense identification with the gangs themselves and, just as inner city gangsters defended their turf, so, too, did the West Coast and East Coast crews defend their regional rap champions. Despite the protests of label heads and their publicists, the bicoastal conflict was very real and increasingly deadly.

Nothing underscored the lethal potential of the rap wars more than the drive-by death of Tupac Shakur in Las Vegas on September 7, 1996. Despite Biggie's enormous popularity, it was Tupac who had been slated for global rap stardom, thanks to his charismatic good looks and intense, driven, and volatile rap style. At the Soul Train Awards, it was Tupac's multi platinum *All Eyez on Me* that would be honored, albeit posthumously, as the year's best album. His murder had thrown into sharp relief the intense rivalry between Puffy Combs' Bad Boy empire and its West Coast counterpart, Death Row Records, owned and operated by the Compton native and one-time UNLV defensive lineman, Marion "Suge" Knight. Just as Biggie was the crown jewel in the Bad Boy roster, Tupac had been Death Row's premier asset. The persistent buzz on the street was that the shooting, still unsolved six months after the fact, was motivated by the ambition of Puffy Combs to rule the rap world by eliminating the competition and establishing East Coast dominance once and for all. While Puffy has seemingly been unwilling to dignify the rumor with a response, a statement he made after another shooting incident targeting Shakur in 1994, in which Puffy was also rumored to be involved, might best sum up his attitude toward such accusations. "This story is beyond ridiculous and completely false," he insisted.

Whether or not Puffy actually had a hand in the rapper's death, Tupac, for his part, provided more than enough provocation. On "Hit 'Em Up," his 1996 single, for example, he attacked the whole East Coast rap establishment, calling out several key figures, including Biggie, Lil Caesar, and Puffy, by name. "Die slow, motherfuckers" he snarled on the song's extended outro. This was something ominously new, even for hard-core gangster rap. On tracks like "Hit 'Em Up" and others, Tupac was doing more than simply joining in the bragging-rights game that most rappers played. He was throwing down the gauntlet, humiliating his rivals in public and all but daring them to come after him.

In this escalating war of words and rhythm, dependable security was more than simply prudent. It was a matter of life and death. But Puffy might have inadvertently ramped up the risk inherent in coming to California by reportedly choosing sides in another long-running gang conflict, this one between L.A.'s notorious Bloods and Crips. While on the West Coast performing on the 1995 Summer Jams tour, Combs was said to have hired Crips to act as bodyguards for stadium stops in Anaheim and San Diego. Among the most prominently and persistently named was Duane Keith Davis, a Compton native known on the streets as "Keffe D," and his nephew, Orlando "Baby Lane" Anderson.

Employing Crips like Keffe D and Baby Lane was another stubborn rumor that Combs dismissed out of hand. "We never used Crips," he asserted to *MTV News,* "or any other gang faction to do security for us." In a subsequent interview, when asked whether he might have been introduced to Keffe D and others without being told they were Crips, Combs insisted, "Being a young black celebrity you have thousands of acquaintances…I can't say who I've met… it's not like all gang people wear colored rags on their heads." But a press agent for his record label was more equivocal. When pressed as to whether it was Biggie who might have, unbeknownst to Puffy, hired Crips as muscle, the publicist responded, "As a family, Bad Boy did not use them," begging the question of who, exactly, was a member of the family.

Perhaps the reason the rumor took root and spread was that such a move would have made a certain kind of sense. Davis and his crew were well-documented, active members in one of Compton's most violent gangs, cold-blooded career thugs, born and bred on the meanest streets of South L.A. If anyone knew the turf, and how to navigate it, it would be Keffe D and his posse.

If Puffy actually had hired Crips as his west coast muscle, he would have put himself squarely in the middle of one of the most violent feuds in American criminal history, the savage war between the Bloods and the Crips. Death Row's mastermind, Suge Knight, had a long and close association with a subset of the Bloods called the Mob Piru. By recruiting Crips for security, Combs would have effectively chosen sides against the Bloods and, more specifically, the Mob Piru, who served as Suge's fiercely loyal enforcers. It's yet another consideration lending credence to the contention that Puffy hired gang members as muscle. "If Death Row is being represented by Bloods," maintains former Tupac Shakur bodyguard Frank Alexander, "it might be understandable to have the rival gang in your employment. It's logical because these guys wouldn't hesitate to fight against the adversary." Under such circumstances, Puffy Combs would have been stepping into a hornet's nest of his own devising and bringing Biggie into it with him.

For his part, Biggie also had security on his mind as he made the rounds of interviews and press appearances in the run-up to the Soul Train festivities. "Rappers' lifestyles should be more protected," he told a reporter from *the Los Angeles Times*, with the recent death of Tupac clearly on his mind. The two had, once upon a time, been close friends. "A drive-by shooting ain't supposed to happen."

The Notorious B.I.G. was himself no stranger to criminal malfeasance. In 1991, he had been arrested in Raleigh, North Carolina, and pled guilty to three counts of drug possession. Four years later, in Camden, New Jersey, he was picked up for robbery and assault. He racked up another assault charge in New York City in 1996, adding to it a count of weapons possession. Biggie had also been followed to Los Angeles by NYPD investigators looking into narcotics and weapons charges as part of a multi-agency grand jury investigation out of Teaneck, New Jersey, where the rapper maintained a palatial home.

Despite the less-than-rapturous reception Biggie and Puffy received at the Soul Train Awards, the rest of the evening had passed without incident. If the rapper was shaken by the catcalls at the Shrine, he didn't show it. He didn't have the time. There were a flurry of details that needed his attention in the days leading up to the release of *Life After Death*. He had initially been set to fly to London for advance promotion of the album, but canceled at the last minute to finish up final touches in the studio. That night he had also agreed to add a verse to "It's All About The Benjamins," a remixed track from Puffy's album *Hell up in Harlem*, a title later changed to *No Way Out*. His busy schedule also included a Vibe magazine interview back at the Westwood Marquee.

While watching the delayed broadcast of the awards show on television, Biggie answered the reporter's questions in his characteristic deep and resonant baritone. He seemed in a particularly thoughtful mood that night, candidly revealing, among other things, his ambivalent feelings toward his estranged wife, Faith Evans.

He had met the Florida singer and songwriter at a photo session when Puffy signed her in 1994 as the first female artist on Bad Boy Records. Nine days later they were married and, in October 1996, they had a son, Christopher Jr. By then, however, the relationship was already falling apart. Biggie regularly stepped out on Evans and had a brief, tempestuous affair with Kimberly "Lil' Kim" Jones, whom he had known from her singing stint with Junior M.A.F.I.A. In fact, one of the more stinging humiliations on Tupac's "Hit 'Em Up" was the rapper's boast that he had had sex with Faith Evans while she was still Biggie's wife.

Biggie's troubled relationship with women was in marked contrast to his utter devotion to his mother, Voletta Wallace. He would call her nearly every day during his L.A. stay, keeping her up-to-date on the latest developments in his whirlwind career. It's hardly surprising, considering that the Jamaican-born Voletta was not only his biggest fan, but had raised him by herself from the age of two. The enduring ghetto tragedy of the absent father—in this case a welder and low-level Jamaican politician named George Latore—created the intense bond between mother and son so common in broken families. It would only be strengthened by Voletta's two bouts with breast cancer and her fervent embrace of Jehovah's Witness doctrine, which, among other tenets, stated that those ascending to heaven after Armageddon would number a strict 144,000.

In her phone conversation with him that night, Voletta expressed surprise that her son was still on the West Coast, instead of on his way to London as planned. He had canceled the trip, he replied, over concerns that U.K. security arrangements were inadequate, but went on to assure her that he was being well protected in Los Angeles. "We have off-duty cops guarding us," he told her, apparently referring to the lone Reggie Blaylock.

Whatever fears and false comforts Biggie may have expressed in his phone call to his mother, they seemed to have faded as the night wore on. Afterward, he and his posse would venture out to take in a late show of *Donnie Brasco*, the Johnny Depp vehicle about a cop infiltrating the mob only to find his identity swallowed up in his assumed life. The early hours of the morning found Biggie back in the studio, working on cuts for Puffy's new album, adding dialogue and imagery from the movie he had just seen, all in his rich, rolling flow.

CHAPTER 2

Incident #7068000030

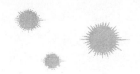

OF ALL THE EVENTS planned in conjunction with the Soul Train Awards that week, none was more eagerly anticipated than the Vibe magazine "after party." If for no other reason than the sheer star power that promised to be in attendance, it was the place to be and be seen. Scheduled for the evening of March 9, the day after the televised presentations, there was only one choice for the gala's venue: 6060 Wilshire Boulevard—The Petersen Automotive Museum.

Vibe was likewise ideally suited to host what promised to be the black entertainment industry's soirée of the season. Launched in 1993 by the influential impresario Quincy Jones in partnership with Time Inc., Vibe had quickly established itself as the voice of the new breed of black artists. It pioneered coverage of rap's astonishing emergence and the escalating controversy that accompanied it, providing extensive coverage on everyone from Snoop Dog and Lil Wayne to 50 Cent and the white rap phenomenon Eminem. The publication would put the full weight of its prestige behind the party, but to ensure that no expense would be spared for the evening, Vibe also enlisted an A-list of co-sponsors, including Tanqueray gin, Tommy Hilfiger clothing, and, for good measure, Quincy Jones's own label, Qwest Records.

Planning for the evening began months beforehand, mostly under the auspices of Vibe's special events coordinator, Karla Radford, who was based in New York. Radford had flown to L.A. to coordinate details with the Petersen staff. She walked the black polished floor of the Grand Salon, laying out seating arrangements and informing the museum's event planners that she expected at least a thousand guests.

That number presented a problem, since capacity for the Grand Salon topped out at only six hundred. A solution was quickly found by securing the first floor gallery space, with room for an additional six hundred to accommodate those further down the celebrity food chain. Additionally, and in keeping with the unending concerns for security that surrounded the Soul Train festivities, Radford retained the services of Da Streetz, Inc. The private protection firm was meant to augment the museum's own security staff, and before the arrangements were complete, yet another guard would be borrowed, from the Natural History Museum.

But in hindsight, Radford's preparations seem woefully inadequate. Even with the addition of another guard, the security contingent totaled a mere ten. What was lacking in manpower would supposedly be made up for by state-of-the-art technology. The museum had several time-lapse surveillance cameras to monitor activities on all four floors, as well as each level of the parking garage, all overseen from a console at the museum's front desk.

Radford, however, seemed more focused on the celebrity contingent than the security contingent. The night before the party, in the midst of the awards program at the Shrine Auditorium, she had circulated among the audience, handing out invitations to any and all of the famous faces she saw. Among those who had the glossy invitation pressed into their hands were the actor Wesley Snipes, the British soul singer Seal, the New York Jets wide receiver Keyshawn Johnson, the Detroit Pistons forward Grant Hill, and a raft of rappers that included Jermaine Dupri, Da Brat, and Heavy D. Before the show was over, she had also managed to buttonhole Puffy Combs and Biggie Smalls.

But Radford was hardly depending on chance encounters to pump up the evening's star quotient. Word of mouth had been spreading for weeks in advance of the Vibe extravaganza. By the time the Petersen opened its doors at 9:00 on a clear dry night with temperatures hovering at a balmy 60 degrees, the turnout was proving to be nothing short of spectacular.

Professional and amateur celebrity spotters, not to mention the LAPD, would later compile and compare lists of attendees that read like a Who's Who of black entertainment, sports, and business. Radford had done this aspect of her work well: it was an impressive showing by any reckoning. In order to check invitations and greet the assorted VIPs, she strategically placed herself at the sweeping glass doors of the museum's entrance, located at the rear of the building. The broad driveway leading to the foyer had access onto both Fairfax and South Orange Grove Avenue, a small semi residential street along the east side of the museum. Its massive overhang, decorated with the flags of auto-manufacturing nations, linked the building directly to its parking structure. Here, limos deposited their passengers while a large and growing crowd of spectators strained at the rope line, their excited shouts greeting each new arrival.

Among the jostling throng were five friends from Houston, Texas who had made the long trip west in a 1982 Chevy 4 x 4 van, specifically to spot stars during the Soul Train celebrations. Devoted rap fans, they had gotten word of the Vibe party and made their way to the Petersen, where they found a bird's-eye view, parked directly across Fairfax Avenue from the museum entrance. They waited expectantly, in hopes of seeing some of their favorite performers.

Despite the mob at the entrance to the Petersen's covered esplanade, they weren't disappointed. Along with such instantly recognizable personalities as the actress Vivica Fox, the Def Jam regular Chris Tucker, the comic siblings Keenan and Marlon Wayans, the NBA superstars Derek Fisher and Jamaal Mashburn, and the soul divas Whitney Houston and Mary J. Blige, invited guests also featured those better known for their rhymes and rhythms than for their faces. As the evening progressed, a contingent of aspiring rap newcomers basked in the flash of cameras and the adoring crowd. Mase, Case, Ginuwine, Missy, Yo Yo, Spinderella, Nefertiti: even these fledging stars arrived with a substantial entourage in tow. The local rapper and Death Row recording artist DJ Quik, for example, was accompanied by a phalanx of no less than a dozen friends and hangers-on, all of whom were duly waved through. The guest list was quickly getting out of control, but there was little Radford could do about it. Everyone had to be afforded the perks of full celebrity status, whether they had earned it yet or not. Who knew which of them might be the next Biggie Smalls?

The man himself, meanwhile, was very nearly a no-show. Worn out from his hectic Los Angeles schedule, Biggie began the day by trying to beg off the event, telling Puffy that he simply wanted to relax and enjoy the California sunshine. As if to underscore the point, he spent most of the rest of the day in the company of Lil' Caesar and Paul Offord at another in the series of Soul Train-related events set for that week; a celebrity charity basketball game at Cal State Dominguez Hills.

It was late that afternoon when he got a call from Puffy. Biggie needed to represent at the Petersen, Combs insisted. He had to show the world that he hadn't been rattled by his reception the previous night at the Soul Train Awards. But it was the networking possibilities afforded by the party that finally brought the rapper around. "Let's go to this Vibe joint," Combs later recalled Biggie saying. "Hopefully, I can meet some people, let them know I want to do some acting." The decision, Combs would assert, "made me proud; he was thinking like a businessman."

But before he could make it to the Petersen, an event promoter from Camden, New Jersey, named Scott Shepherd buttonholed Biggie in his suite at the Westwood Marquee. A whole different kind of businessman, Shepherd was one of the swarm of opportunists operating at the fringes of the entertainment industry. He had tailed Biggie to California, intent on pitching a bizarre scheme to celebrate the star's birthday with a series of parties across the country.

Arriving at the hotel with Shepherd was another would-be entertainment entrepreneur looking to cash in on Biggie's fame. Ernest "Troia" Anderson was a freelance screenwriter desperate to make a feature film biography of the rapper under the auspices of Bad Boy Films, a division of Puffy's empire that as yet existed only on paper. Teaming up with his colleague Shepherd, they had driven to the Westwood Marquee in Anderson's 1995 white Toyota Land Cruiser, a vehicle that would play an unlikely role in the chaotic events about to unfold.

Shepherd and Anderson managed to attach themselves to Biggie and his posse as they left the hotel that evening in a convoy composed of two green Chevy Suburbans and a black Blazer, all 1997 model year rentals. The hapless duo followed in Anderson's vehicle, assuming they were on their way to the Vibe party as special guests of the Notorious B.I.G. Instead they wound their way up into the Hollywood Hills above Sunset Strip, arriving at a sumptuous mansion owned by Andre Harrell, founder of Uptown Records. Harrell had given Puffy his first big break in the music business and now had lent Combs the plush spread for the duration of his stay of Los Angeles.

Puffy was waiting, ready to get the evening started, and neither Shepherd nor Anderson had a chance to pitch their respective schemes before the caravan got rolling again. They followed close behind, relishing their new roles as privileged players in Biggie's inner circle.

It was a big circle. Eleven men accompanied the rap star that night. Along with Puffy and Lil' Caesar, the group included an assortment of childhood friends, aspiring rappers, and business associates. The security contingent was headed by Ken Story, Reggie Blaylock, and Paul Offord, who oversaw a squad of Bad Boy bodyguards composed of Gregory "G-Money" Young, Damien "D-Roc" Butler, and Lewis "Groovy Lew" Jones, as well as Eugene Deal, Steve Jordan, and Anthony Jacobs.

Arriving shortly after 9:30, just as the party was getting under way, Biggie, Puffy, and company, with Shepherd and Anderson slipping in alongside, were greeted with a blinding barrage of photoflashes. The spontaneous roar from the crowd was easily the loudest of the evening. At Karla Radford's signal, the doors swung wide and they were escorted to the second-floor Grand Salon, their security detail plowing through the crush of ogling partygoers that were already starting to fill the ground-floor galleries.

While Biggie usually favored boxy, three-piece designer suits topped by an expensive felt bowler hat, he was making a different, and decidedly more downplayed, fashion statement for the occasion, dressed in faded blue jeans and a black velour shirt. He also sported sunglasses and the gold-headed cane he had been using since the car accident that shattered his left leg during the recording of *Life After Death*. A large gold medallion etched with the face of Jesus was hung around his neck, replacing his usual pendant, which featured the branded Bad Boy icon of a glowering baby in a baseball cap and construction boots.

Biggie Smalls and Puffy Combs at the Peterson VIBE party, March 9, 1997, shortly before Biggie was gunned down. *Photo Credit:BlackImages Archives*

God and religion had, it seemed, been much on Biggie's mind in recent weeks. He had worn a conspicuous crucifix to the Soul Train awards and while in L.A. had gotten a tattoo for the first and only time, choosing a lengthy passage from Psalms 27 rendered as a scroll of tattered parchment on his massive forearm. *"The Lord is my light and my salvation,"* the ink read, *"whom shall I fear? The Lord is the truth of my life, of whom shall I be afraid? When the wicked, even my enemies and foes, came upon me to bite my flesh, they stumbled and fell."*

Exaltation and excitement greeted him as he made his entrance into the Grand Salon, taking a ringside seat in a corner booth beside the dance floor as the DJ slipped "Hypnotize" onto the turntable at full volume. It would be played eight more times consecutively, and at frequent intervals thereafter, as the rapper received the honors and accolades of the crowd. He beamed happily, sipping Cristal champagne and taking hits on the pungent blunts that were passed his way. Women would break from the mobbed floor to dance seductively before him, and a raft of celebrities dropped by to bask in his glow. Among the many was Russell Simmons, the pioneering founder of Def Jam Records.

"He was sitting there," Simmons would later recall, "not even moving his cane. He was so cool, so funny and calm. I wanted to be like him." It's revealing that Simmons, a towering figure in modern black music, would find himself awestruck in the presence of the young rapper. But this was Biggie's night and there was no denying him his due.

Under the circumstances, it seems unlikely that he would have been aware of troubling undercurrents amid all the attention and excitement. Mingling with the glittering guests were clusters of Crips and Bloods, sworn enemies who might or might not have put their differences aside for the evening. The fact was, the presence of authentic thugs only added to the evening's edgy glamour. The posse that accompanied DJ Quik, for example, turned out to be fully-fledged members of the Tree Top Piru, the Bloods from Compton's north side. Among the more notable Crips in attendance were Duane Keith "Keffe D," Davis and his nephew "Baby Lane" Anderson. They had also arrived with a delegation of more than a dozen gangbangers.

For the most part the rivals merely glowered at each other across the dance floor and down the length of the bar. Meanwhile, out on Wilshire Boulevard and Fairfax Avenue, even more gang members were milling around, looking for a way into the action. A security guard on the payroll of Da Streetz was stationed at the Fairfax entrance, where he was instructed to turn away the overflow by any means available. The best he could come up with on the spot was the feeble excuse that they were wearing tennis shoes, in violation of an imaginary dress code. But as the partying continued without incident, it seemed to some observers that a sort of unspoken truce had taken effect. The thugs were under control, there to provide local color and nothing more.

It was not an opinion shared by Keffe D. It would have been hard not to notice the Crip's hulking, intimidating presence hovering at Biggie's corner table. But whatever the purpose of the whispered conversation Keffe D was having with Puffy Combs, nothing but the slight whistling through his gapped front teeth could be heard over the pounding bass of the music. The party rolled on and the crowd got bigger. The crush on the first and second floors quickly doubled Radford's original estimate of a thousand, and still more guests, invited or otherwise, were pushing themselves past the heavy glass doors and the increasingly overwhelmed security contingent.

The situation was rapidly reaching critical mass. As early as ten o'clock, museum guards had made a futile attempt to clear the front entrance. The crowd pushed back, their mood growing progressively surlier as they heard the thudding party mix just beyond their reach inside the Petersen.

An hour later, a fire marshal from the L.A. Fire Department's station 52, who had been on the scene the entire evening to monitor possible safety violations, put in a radio summons to the LAPD Wilshire Division for help with crowd control. After twenty minutes the police arrived, surveyed the scene, and decided the best course of action would be to let the event run its course rather than risk stirring up an angry mob. They left.

At that point, a sequence of confusing and contradictory events started to cascade. As midnight approached, the fire marshal decided that he had no choice but to try to shut the event down. "This party is over!" a fireman announced over a bullhorn on the first floor. "Please leave immediately in an orderly manner."

The crowd reacted with angry shouts, both inside and outside the museum, as word quickly spread upstairs that the evening was coming to an early conclusion. Slowly departing guests ran directly into the throng of fans still waiting outside on the off chance of getting in. The entrance to the museum quickly became a logjam and except for the ten frightened security guards, there was no one on the scene to enforce the evacuation.

At 12:05 A.M., the desperate fire marshal made his way to the Petersen's front desk, where video monitors displayed the premises from several different angles. He ordered the guard who manned the desk to put in another call to the Wilshire Division. Not only had the crowd become uncontrollable, there were now scattered reports of a shot being fired from a black Ford Bronco seen heading south on Orange Grove Avenue. Eyewitnesses had gotten the license plate number. As the guard speed-dialed the Wilshire Division, he looked through the glass doors of the entrance, where several panicked people were running and ducking.

Meanwhile, Biggie and Puffy were making their way leisurely down from the Grand Salon. Ken Story, G-Money, and Reggie Blaylock hurried ahead to bring around the cars as the rest of the posse formed a protective phalanx around the stars. At that point, the plan was to head out to a private after-after-party at the home of a record company executive. But it was going to be awhile before they got there. Biggie's still-mending leg was aching, making it painful to move through the fans who repeatedly waylaid him, wanting photos and autographs. It took nearly forty minutes to reach the front entrance of the museum, where the unruly mob was still refusing to disperse.

Biggie and his cohort stood at the valet stand on Fairfax waiting for their SUV's, which had pulled out of the parking garage and were idling less than a block away. As they headed for their rides, the rapper turned back to some friends. "See y'all at the next party," he said, his voice barely audible above the turmoil.

But as they moved down the street, Biggie and Puffy decided to call it a night. They had wanted to squeeze in more studio time the next morning. It was still early enough to get a solid night's sleep and be fresh for the session. The group divided. Combs climbed into the front passenger seat of the first Suburban, driven by Ken Story. The bodyguards Eugene Deal, Steve Jordan, and Anthony Jacobs clambered into the backseats.

Biggie took the second of the matching green SUV's. On its rear bumper a sticker read Think B.I.G. March 25, 1997, a teaser for the upcoming *Life After Death* album. Riding shotgun beside G-Money, Biggie was joined in the vehicle by Lil Caesar, D-Roc and Groovy Lew Jones. At the wheel of the Blazer, the last vehicle in the line, was Reggie Blaylock, who shared the front seat with Paul Offord.

The convoy pulled into the northbound lane of Fairfax and started to cross Wilshire Boulevard. As the GMC with Puffy aboard moved into the intersection, the stoplight turned yellow and Ken Story accelerated quickly to get to the far side. Behind them, G-Money pulled to a stop at the red light, the Suburban's stereo pounding out a track from *Life After Death*.

From that moment on, the events at the corner of Fairfax and Wilshire, shortly after 12:30 on the morning of March 9, 1997, disintegrated into a dozen distinct points of view, each reflecting a different perspective.

It's a common perception that the facts of any crime can be established by a careful correlation of forensic evidence and eyewitness accounts. Yet, more often than not, forensic findings collapse into a welter of incongruous and mutually exclusive data, and eyewitness testimony is worse than useless. Memory, at best, is unreliable. Perceptions can be colored and warped by presumption, emotion, and all the intangible circumstances of the moment.

At no time was that principle more in play than in the events leading up to the murder of Christopher Wallace. Who saw what, in what sequence and from what viewpoint, depended in large part on who they were, what they thought they had seen, and what they

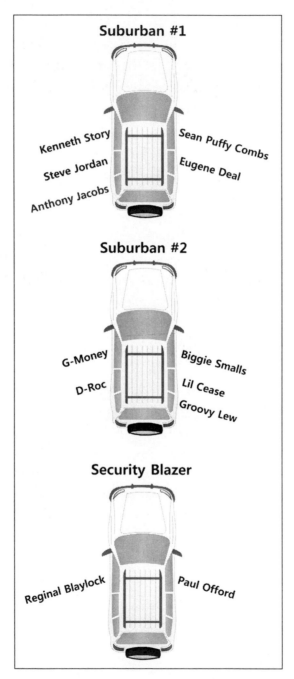

Biggie Smalls' entourage and vehicle configuration.
Illustration by C. Jackson Investigations Inc.

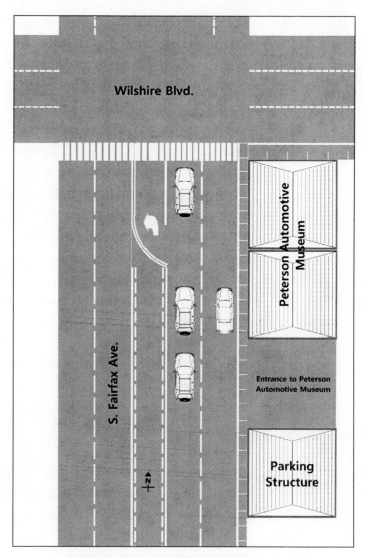

Approximate location of vehicles at time of shooting.
Illustration by C. Jackson Investigations Inc.

wanted others to believe they had seen. The scene at the Petersen was sheer pandemonium, packed with eyewitnesses, innocent bystanders and curious gawkers. Time lines overlapped and diverged at several key points, speeding up or slowing down according to what each witness considered important. There were those who, caught in the frenzied mob, had no idea what was happening; others who, with their own agendas and inside information, were sure they knew exactly what was going down and why. And somewhere in between were the police, frantically trying to make sense of a still unfolding situation.

One of the jagged puzzle pieces that authorities would later try to fit into a coherent whole was the view of the rap fans from Houston, who had parked across Fairfax earlier that evening. Watching the departures of the celebrities as the party began slowly and reluctantly to break up, one of the six began videotaping the scene. It was at that point that they would later recall hearing a screech of tires coming rapidly up behind them. A moment later six shots, three equally spaced and three in quick succession, can be heard on the grainy video footage.

"Somebody got shot!" a voice says from the back of the van.

"It was Biggie!" another shouts.

"No, it was Puff!" a third insists.

"Somebody got shot!" the first voice, now shaking with fear, says again.

The audio track garbles, the camera swings wildly, and the image pixelates. "Y'all crank up the car, please," a girl's voice pleads. "I'm ready to go."

Moments before, a group of four women had made their way from the choked museum entrance and were headed north on Fairfax toward Wilshire, in the same direction as Biggie's departing convoy. They were Aysha Foster, Selma Jefferson, Shala King, and Inga Marchand, better known as the rapper Foxy Brown.

The four had flown in from Brooklyn to attend the Soul Train awards. As the Vibe party began degenerating, the foursome, all of whom had some connection to the music industry, had decided to beat a retreat to yet another after-party. Foster, the fiancée of Biggie's associate D-Roc, worried that her husband-to-be would find out she was on the town without him and was hurrying toward Foxy

Brown's gold Lexus 300 parked near a fire hydrant on Fairfax Avenue. Before she reached the vehicle, Foster heard the same screeching of tires and rapid report of gunfire. Almost immediately, she saw a southbound white SUV make a sharp U-turn and try to squeeze in behind the second Suburban and the black Blazer, driven by Reggie Blaylock. The off-duty cop lurched forward, cutting off access, and the white SUV swerved back into the southbound lane, speeding away down Fairfax.

Meanwhile, a security guard on the graveyard shift at the Petersen had arrived to work on a Wilshire Boulevard bus. Coming in through the relatively quiet staff entrance, he went to the locker room, where he changed into his uniform and reported for duty. He was immediately directed up to the second floor to help clear the Grand Salon of lingering guests. In the process of emptying the huge space, he stepped onto the balcony that opened up off the Grand Salon with a spectacular view of the Miracle Mile. "I just heard gunshots," said an unknown voice behind him, although the guard himself had not heard the firing. He moved to the edge of the balcony and looked down, just as black-and-whites began pulling up, sirens howling.

The police had finally arrived in response to the latest request for assistance from the beleaguered Petersen, where the single shot fired from a Ford Bronco on Orange Grove Avenue had been reported. Even as they were moving out, another call was received. It was 12:35. More shots had been heard, semiautomatic gunfire this time, coming now from the west side of the museum, on Fairfax Avenue.

Sergeant Gary Fredo of the Wilshire Division, receiving the urgent summons, generated an Incident Number: 7068000030. Joining the units just then rolling out, Fredo arrived at a scene of complete bedlam. The crowd was hostile, refusing to leave even as the gunshots had left them fearful and apprehensive. The arrival of the police only heightened the tense atmosphere, and beer cans began flying. "I formed a skirmish line of officers," Fredo would later report, "and entered the location. We needed to find the Fire Department personnel and make an attempt at controlling a possible crime scene."

"There were people in the crowd," Fredo continued, "who refused to move or attempted to push their way past the skirmish line. They exhibited unlawful, hostile behavior and did not respond to verbal directions to disperse. It was impossible to arrest these individuals at the time, due to the officers being outnumbered. After approximately forty minutes, and with the use of approximately sixty uniformed police officers, we were finally able to gain control of the situation."

It was only then that the authorities began trying to sort out what exactly had happened. Were the two reports of gunfire related? Were they even separate incidents? Was the black Bronco on Orange Grove Avenue and the white SUV that made a sudden 360 somehow part of a coordinated attack? And, more to the point, who, if anyone, had actually been shot?

The answer to that last question was, at that moment, lying on an operating table at Cedars Sinai Hospital, gasping for air as his chest cavity filled with blood. With all the conflicting information, rumor, and speculation surrounding that night, there would remain one piece of irrefutable evidence: the six-foot-three, 360-pound corpse of Biggie Smalls.

CHAPTER 3

Mad Dogging

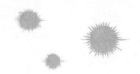

BIGGIE HAD DIED AS HE LIVED: surrounded by an entourage, even if, this time, it had been randomly gathered from the war zone around the Petersen. Puffy Combs, who in the moments immediately following the shooting was the first at Biggie's side, would lead the deathwatch.

It was Combs who had shouted at the driver, Ken Story, to slow down, halfway across Wilshire Boulevard, as the shots rang out behind them and everyone in the vehicle reflexively ducked. Story glanced up into the rearview mirror and saw Biggie's Suburban stopped at the light across the intersection.

He immediately made a U-turn and pulled up directly in front of the idling SUV. Combs jumped out, ran to the vehicle, and opened the passenger door. There was a look of surprise on the victim's face, as if he couldn't quite believe what had just happened. "I was trying to talk to him," Combs would later recount. "But he wasn't saying

anything or hearing anything." Distraught, Puffy had tried to pull
the dying man from the car, aided by a few bystanders. But it was
futile: Biggie's massive frame was, literally and figuratively, dead
weight. Instead, Puffy got back into the Suburban, peremptorily
ordering Eugene Deal, who had replaced Ken Story behind the wheel,
to drive to the nearest hospital, without waiting for an ambulance to
be summoned or the police to arrive. Story, meanwhile, had taken
over driving from G-Money in the death car and followed Deal up
Wilshire Boulevard with the mortally wounded Biggie beside him.
He had still not uttered a word.

Meanwhile, from the front seat of the black Blazer, the last car
in the convoy, Paul Offord and Reggie Blaylock had gotten the best
view of what had happened. Just prior to the shooting, moving up
to take their place as the follow-up vehicle, they were momentarily
distracted by the white SUV trying to squeeze in front of them. As
Blaylock hurried to close the gap and cut off the interloper, the six
shots rang out. Acting on long experience as a police officer in gang-
infested Inglewood, Blaylock ducked beneath the dash, then quickly
looked up again to mark where the gunfire was coming from.

As he would later recall, with a cop's eye for detail "I saw a 1994
or '95 Chevrolet Impala, SS, black, with large wide tires, possibly
eighteen inches, stopped in the northbound number two lane next
to Biggie's car. It was about twenty-five feet in front of me. I saw
the driver holding a gun with his right hand extended out the open
window. I never saw the driver's face, only his hand. I can say only
the color of the hand was lighter than mine. I heard Paul Offord
saying from the passenger seat beside me, "Right there! Right there!
Someone is shooting!"

The Impala peeled off onto Wilshire Boulevard, accelerating
east. Blaylock gave chase. The pursuit was cut short, however, due to
a built-in gasoline governor in the rented Blazer, which decreased the
fuel supply if the car exceeded ninety miles an hour. Blaylock soon

lost sight of the fleeing vehicle, which had turned down one of the dimly lit side streets off Wilshire, and he returned to the crime scene.

For his part, Offord had been distracted by the sudden appearance of the white SUV in the last moments before the shooting. "I think it might have been involved," he later told police, recalling how, as the shots rang out, the mysterious car had vanished south on Fairfax.

Minutes later, as he floored the Suburban up Wilshire Boulevard on his way to the hospital, Ken Story would have had time to consider how it had all gone so wrong. As owner and operator of T.N.T. Protection Services, he had utterly failed to carry out his primary responsibility, to keep his client alive. There were going to be fingers pointed, that much was for sure, and he was equally sure they would be pointed in his direction.

In retrospect, the entire night at the Petersen had seemed to Story full of ominous portents. "After the party," he would later tell police, "while standing in the parking structure, I noticed a lone male several feet away, staring at us. I signaled to Damien Butler that we should keep an eye on him. He appeared to be a gang member, dark complexion, wearing blue jeans and a white striped shirt. I think he could have been involved in Biggie's death because of the way he was mad dogging us."

But Story's recollections and recriminations were cut short as he made the desperate dash, up Wilshire to San Vicente Boulevard, then north a short distance to the emergency room entrance of Cedars-Sinai Medical Center. A hysterical woman, perched in the backseat next to Biggie, was alternately screaming directions to the medical center and a stream of profanities directed at everyone on the guard detail, particularly Bad Boy's security chief, Paul Offord.

It was Aysha Foster, one of the four women who had been in close proximity to the shooting as they walked down Wilshire Boulevard. Foster, whose only connection to Biggie was her impending marriage to his friend D-Roc, crouched behind Foxy Brown's Lexus with her friends as the bullets flew. A short distance from where the women were hiding, the Impala sped off just as Foster raised her head to see Puffy standing at the bullet-punctured door of Biggie's car. She hurried across the street, dodging the black Blazer as it gave chase, and jumped into the Suburban just as Ken Story was pulling away behind the SUV carrying Combs. There she gave full-throated expression to the anger, fear, and outrage felt by everyone. "I remember thinking to myself that she was someone close to Biggie," Story would recall; "a sister, a relative, or a close friend."

Ken Story wouldn't be the only one replaying the evening's events. For James "Lil' Caesar" Lloyd, there was more than enough second-guessing to occupy him all the way to the hospital. In retrospect, the threat to his cousin and musical mentor had been clear enough during the Vibe party. First and foremost, there was the presence of Duane "Keffe D" Davis, the Crip kingpin Puffy had previously turned to for West Coast security. Keffe D had buttonholed Combs for a whispered exchange at Biggie's ringside table, but at the time Lil' Caesar had no idea what the conversation was about. It was only after the fire marshal had announced that the party was over and the entourage was on its way out that he heard firsthand what was on Keffe D's mind.

"Hey, man," Lil' Caesar recalled Davis saying to him, some twenty minutes before the shooting. "You need some security, someone on your side ..." Lloyd, who had met the Crip a year earlier backstage at a Combs Summer Jam concert in Anaheim, assured him that everything was under control. He gave little thought to Keffe-D's offer of additional muscle. It had seemed, at the time, like just another hustle.

It must not have seemed that way in the immediate aftermath of the shooting. Perhaps Davis had been trying to tell him something. Perhaps he could have warned him of the light-complexioned black man with the receding hairline, wearing an incongruous bow tie, that Lil Caesar had glimpsed in the driver's seat of the Impala, firing away at the helpless bulk of his cousin?

Eugene Deal, part of the Bad Boy security detail, might well have been rehearsing his own misgivings as he drove Puff to the hospital, flat out down the six-lane boulevard. Deal had accompanied Biggie and Combs to the Soul Train awards the night before and stayed behind with Puffy after the rapper, rattled by the hostile reception, had left immediately after the presentation. It was backstage at the Shrine that Deal overheard a brief encounter between Combs and Mustapha Farrakhan, the son of the Nation of Islam's controversial leader, Louis Farrakhan, and a close acquaintance of the star.

The tense exchange began when an unknown member of the organization had stepped in front of Combs as he was leaving by the stage door. "I want to talk to you," he said, in a characteristically clipped Black Muslim manner. "You are disrespecting our brothers in the east."

Deal had no idea what the issue might be, but remembered Combs turning to Farrakhan, standing nearby. "Yo, Mustapha," he entreated. "Tell him you and I are cool." Farrakhan nodded to his lieutenant, who stepped back and let Combs pass. The standoff had ended as quickly as it began.

Or had it? After the party at the Petersen, as Deal waited for Puffy and Biggie to say their goodbyes, he noticed an individual walking quickly up Fairfax. Light-skinned, with a sparse mustache and a receding hairline, he was wearing a blue suit and a bow tie, the trademark attire of the Nation of Islam.

It was only later that Deal would discover that his description, at least in part, matched those of others who had caught a glimpse of the shooter behind the wheel of the Impala. Foremost among them: Gregory "G-Money" Young.

Driving the second Suburban, G-Money had turned in time to see a black man in a bow tie, left hand on the steering wheel, and the glint of a gun in his right. Lil' Caesar would subsequently report much the same thing to police when describing the glimpse he had gotten of the killer through the open window of the Impala. He had a fade haircut, Lil' Caesar would recall, and was wearing a light-colored suit and a bow tie, although it was hard to tell in the glare of the streetlights in the intersection.

Was Biggie's death in retaliation by the Black Muslims for some slight, real or imagined, that Combs had committed against the "brothers in the east?" To Eugene Deal, it seemed a distinct possibility. He wouldn't be the only one to eventually connect those circumstantial dots.

It took a little more than five minutes for the two vehicles to reach the hospital. They screeched to a stop at the emergency room entrance, halfway down a short street bisecting the sprawling medical facility. It was shortly before 1:00 a.m. D-Roc was the first out, jumping from the still-rolling SUV and running headlong into the lobby, shouting for assistance. He led a pair of paramedics back to the car, opening the door on Biggie's inert body. After a look at the size of the victim, one of the emergency room staff hurried back in to get more help. It eventually took six men to hoist Biggie out of the seat and onto a waiting gurney.

Conspicuous in its absence was the blood that should have been gushing from the massive wounds the rapper had sustained. In fact, Biggie was so padded with fat that the paths of the bullets simply closed up, blocking off the blood flow. All the hemorrhaging was occurring internally.

Biggie showed no signs of life, and it was later determined that he probably expired at the scene of the shooting. Yet the emergency staff still undertook a heroic effort to resuscitate him. For twenty minutes, doctors in the trauma center performed an emergency thoracotomy, internal defibrillations, and eventually a last-ditch intracardiac massage.

Meanwhile, in the ER lobby, Combs was on his knees, praying for the life of his friend. Lil' Caesar lay beside him on the linoleum floor, sobbing uncontrollably. The harshly lit room was slowly filling up with others who had rushed over from the Petersen, including Biggie's estranged wife, Faith Evans. Some gathered in small clusters, hands joined in prayer, wiping away inconsolable tears. Others simply sat staring at the waiting room artwork that hung on the cream-colored walls.

After what some would remember as an eternity and others recall as the blink of an eye, a doctor approached Combs and Evans. Christopher Wallace, he told them, was gone. He had been pronounced dead at 1:15 a.m.

A stunned silence followed, punctuated by the sobs of Evans and Foster. A tentative discussion began among Biggie's closest confidants as to who would inform his mother. It was D-Roc who finally made the call, reaching Voletta Wallace in her Brooklyn home at 5:21 EST. He could hardly speak through choking sobs and Voletta, immediately fearing the worst, let out a piercing scream. Her sister-in-law, who was staying with her at the time, took the phone and eventually coaxed the grim news from D-Roc, informing the prostrate mother of what she already knew.

As dawn broke that morning, Voletta Wallace was already on her way to the airport for the flight to Los Angeles to indentify her son and make preparations to bring his body home. By that time, news of the rapper's death had already been flashed across the country and around the world. Radio stations began a nonstop rotation of his music and record outlets put in urgent calls to distributors, upping their orders for *Life After Death*.

By dying in a spectacular burst of violence, Wallace had, in fact, become even larger than he had been in life. And almost as quickly a flood of speculations, rumors and conspiracy theories began circulating, gaining credence with each retelling.

While the motive for the murder was anyone's—and everyone's—guess, the cold facts of the homicide were left for the deputy medical examiner, Dr. Lisa Scheinin, to detail during the autopsy performed that morning at 10:30. She determined "multiple gunshot wounds to the abdomen and chest" as the official cause of death. Four of the six bullets fired from the Impala had found their mark, one each in the left forearm, the soft tissue of the back, and the muscle of the left thigh, all non-fatal. The fourth was a different matter. Its trajectory had successively penetrated the ascending colon, the liver, the pericardium, the heart, and the upper lobe of the left lung. This fatal, final bullet finally came to rest in the victim's anterior left shoulder, where it was recovered by the coroner. In the course of her detailed examination, Scheinin would also note that the victim was morbidly obese and had a long biblical inscription tattooed on his right forearm. For the purpose of the procedure, a toe tag confirmed his identity.

Eight days later, Biggie's body lay in state at the viewing parlor of the Frank E. Campbell Funeral Home on Madison Avenue on Manhattan's Upper East Side. His remains filled a large mahogany coffin lined in white velvet, open to reveal his head and upper torso. He had been dressed in a cream-colored double-breasted suit and matching shirt, a teal blue tie, and a white derby hat.

Outside, along Madison Avenue, thousands of fans had gathered, holding up posters of the slain rapper and playing his music on boom boxes at full volume. Inside, 350 invited guests sat through a ceremony dubbed the *"Final Tour."* Puffy Combs delivered the eulogy and Faith Evans performed the gospel classic "Walk with Me, Lord." The recessional was an instrumental version of "Miss U," a song Biggie had written after the death of Tupac Shakur. *"The motherfuckin' shit just get me so motherfuckin' mad,"* read the unsung lyrics, *"'cause you know that was my nigger."*

The guest list for the service was, in its own way, even more impressive than the all-star roster at the disastrous Vibe party. Aside from Puffy, his substantial Bad Boy posse, all the members of Junior M.A.F.I.A., and a sizeable contingent of Wallace's extended family, the mourners included Mary J. Blige, Queen Latifah, Dr. Dre,

Sister Souljah, Mustapha Farrakhan, Tommy Hilfiger, Flavor Flav, Lauren Hill, Wyclef Jean, Naomi Campbell, Kweisi Mfume of the NAACP head, the former New York City mayor David Dinkins, Congresswoman Maxine Waters, and rappers including Q-Tip and DJ Clark Kent. Also on the invited list, buried among the celebrity well wishers, was the name Robert Ross, known on the streets of South Central LA as "Stutterbox."

As the funeral motorcade moved down FDR Drive, over the Brooklyn Bridge and into the heart of Biggie's old stomping grounds, crowds lined the streets of Fort Greene, Clinton Hill, and Bedford-Stuyvesant. Along the route, impromptu shrines of flowers, candles, and malt liquor bottles had been laid out, as well as street vendors peddling assorted Notorious B.I.G. memorabilia. The distinctive sound of Biggie's raps echoed from windows as the hearse proceeded at a stately pace to the Fresh Ponds Crematory in Middle Village, Queens.

But what should have been a solemn farewell quickly turned violent as spectators clashed with a heavy police presence. Riot-equipped SWAT teams, who had taken up position at various key points along the route, used nightsticks and pepper spray to disperse the increasingly unruly onlookers. By the time the motorcade finally rolled through the wide gate of the crematorium, ten people had been arrested, with several more suffering minor injuries.

In the memorial service program, Voletta Wallace had expressed her gratitude to "the people she hasn't met yet who've lent their support, given their positive feedback and helped her remain strong through this difficult time." But as she took the ashes of her son home that afternoon, there was another group already beginning to come together, a loosely linked network of police investigators, gang associates, and amateur sleuths of every description, determined to find out who had killed Christopher Wallace, and why.

PART
TWO

CHAPTER 4

The Call

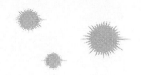

ON MAY 1, 2006, a little more than nine years after the events at the Petersen Automotive Museum, I received a call from Detective Brian Tyndall of the Los Angeles Police Department's Robbery-Homicide Division. He asked if I would be interested in becoming part of a task force charged with reopening the Biggie Smalls murder investigation. I remember the date: the department was on maximum deployment in anticipation of May Day demonstrations. It was also my birthday.

My name is Greg Kading. At the time I took the call, I was a detective supervisor assigned to the LAPD's Major Narcotics Unit. I understood immediately why I was being asked to work on a case that, while it had long since gone cold, was still one of the most famous unsolved murders in the annals of American criminal justice. I was, to put it as modestly as possible, well qualified for the job. It was almost as if everything I'd accomplished in law enforcement up until then had been in preparation for this single assignment.

On the other hand, my whole career could also be considered an unlikely choice for someone of my background. I was born in Reno, Nevada, where my parents worked in the casinos and divorced when I was two years old. It was the sixties and my mother, who was very much a child of those times, hit the road with my two older sisters and me in tow. Over the next decade we lived like gypsies, moving from house to house, sometimes campground to campground, never staying in one place for long. I attended school only sporadically and was slipped my first dose of LSD at age ten, courtesy of one of my mom's hippie friends. A year later we headed south to Mexico, where my mother's boyfriend had scored a few kilos of cocaine. The plan was to meet up with him and head back to the States in the guise of an innocent family of tourists. We got as far as Orange County, California, before word came that the federales had nabbed the would-be dope runner. With no place left to go, we just stayed where we were.

It was in the town of San Juan Capistrano that we settled into what passed for a normal life. I joined a Pop Warner football team, whose coach, Wyatt Hart, a lieutenant in the Orange County Sheriff's Department, became in many important ways the father I never had. I was sixteen when my mother once again decided to move on. I refused to go and the coach offered to take me in. Realizing she couldn't provide the stability I craved, my mom agreed. Over the next few years I became for all intents and purposes a member of the coach's family. He was the one who guided me, gently but persuasively, toward a career in law enforcement, using his influence to help me land a job with the Sheriff's Department in 1986.

As a sheriff's deputy, I was assigned various tasks within the county's jail system and, while it hardly suited my image of actual police work, it was there that I first gained a working knowledge of criminals and criminal mentality. Nevertheless, I had no intention of spending my days shuttling inmates to court dates or conducting cell searches. Instead, I applied to the LAPD and was accepted, graduating from the academy in March 1989.

My first assignment was as a patrol officer in the Newton Division in South Los Angeles. Covering a large swath of downtown LA, Newton was in the hotly contested heart of the city's raging gang war zone. As a beat cop on those tense and dangerous streets, I gained firsthand familiarity with the infrastructure of more than thirty active gangs, constructing elaborate flow charts detailing the hierarchy of the Four-Trey Crips and the Five-Deuce Gangster Crips, the Blood Stone Villains and the Hang Out Boys. The list went on and I made it my business to familiarize myself with each faction, their turf boundaries and the specifics of the specialized criminal enterprises that kept them in business.

There was an intense sense of camaraderie among the officers at Newton. It's that feeling of loyalty, to your partners, your division and to the department as a whole, that I believe is essential to an effective police force. We shared a common sense of purpose and, more important, had one another's backs. The men and women I worked with were more than colleagues, even more than friends. They were individuals who one day might be called upon to save my life and vice versa. That's a powerful bond. In the rising tide of gang activity that, by the early nineties, would all but overwhelm the city, we saw ourselves as society's last stand against total anarchy. But it was more than just the performance of our sworn duties. There was an undeniably daring aspect to chasing bad guys, putting your life on the line, and swapping stories with your buddies over a beer at the end of a long day. I loved being a cop. I loved being a good guy. And I loved it when the good guys won.

I didn't share that sense of solidarity nearly as much when, in early 1990, I was transferred to the Wilshire Division in the LAPD's West Bureau. At that time Wilshire was simmering with racial tensions among black, white, and Hispanic officers. It wouldn't have been noticeable to a casual observer, but in the locker rooms or after-hour hangouts, a clear division was discernible among the ranks. It made me uncomfortable, but I kept my head down and my nose clean, and after a few months I was recruited back to Newton to become part of a unit called Community Resources Against Street Hoodlums: CRASH, for short.

Formed in the early seventies by the legendary and controversial police chief Daryl Gates, CRASH was charged with stemming the tide of gang violence fueled primarily by the drug trade. Given unprecedented freedom of action, CRASH showed results, especially during 1987's Operation Hammer, a citywide sweep of gang hideouts that accounted for nearly fifteen hundred arrests on a single weekend in April of that year. Given the crisis atmosphere of the time, with drive-by shootings causing tragic collateral damage on an almost daily basis, it was easy to justify the free hand that CRASH had been afforded. But with it, inevitably, came accusations of abuse and overreaching.

I'd be the first to admit that CRASH used questionable methods to get the job done. In 1992, the world was shocked when the videotaped beating of Rodney King was aired. Within CRASH, such manhandling of known gang members was standard operating procedure. Prior to the King uproar, car chases in the city were a relatively rare occurrence. The simple fact was that most gangsters knew exactly what would happen to them once they were run to ground. After the King incident, vehicle pursuits became a regular occurrence as criminals confronted a police department battered with charges of brutality and racism.

CRASH would itself crash and burn in the late nineties when a major scandal erupted out of the Rampart Division's CRASH unit. But I have to say that during my time as a CRASH officer, a lot got done to clean up the streets. Angelinos were united in their terror of a virtual gang takeover, and CRASH was an appropriate response to that crisis. Our morale was high and our mission was clear. With CRASH on the streets—becoming in the words of one observer, "the most badass gang in the city"—thugs and, more important, innocent bystanders stopped dying in their dozens.

Over a five-year period my performance was such that I was singled out to become part of a federally run task force focusing on organized gang activity, particularly the vicious Bloodstone Villains Gang operating out of South Central L.A. At that time, gang turf was pretty much divided right down the middle by the 110, with those on one side of the freeway using the Westside designation, while those on the other were considered "East Coast."

For me, the real value of working with the federal task force, personally and professionally, was in learning the nuances of inter-agency collaboration. Although I was still operating out of Newton, I was under federal auspices, which meant that I learned up close how lines of authority are established, resources are allocated, and, most important, how turf battles are overcome so that information and manpower can be effectively shared. After four years on the federal task force, I was promoted to detective and reassigned back to the Wilshire Division, where I was naturally given more gang work. It was there that I met a young homicide investigator named Daryn Dupree and realized just how much I still had to learn about the criminal subculture we were both battling.

Smart, professional, and an impeccable dresser to boot, Daryn was born and raised by a single mother in South Central Los Angeles, the heart of Crips territory. There were major drug dealers in his extended family, and Daryn quickly learned how to navigate the ghetto streets, instinctively turning to sports to stay out of gang life. At the same time he developed a deep appreciation for rap music, hearing in it an authentic expression of the streets he knew only too well. Urged on by his mother, he joined the LAPD and was assigned to the Wilshire Division. The truth is, I have never met anyone, inside or outside the force, who understood as much about L.A.'s black gangs—the major players, the economic base, the hierarchies and pecking orders—than Daryn Dupree.

Naturally, given his wealth of inside knowledge, Dupree was eventually selected for the Wilshire Division's CRASH unit. During his tenure, he expanded his grasp of gangs and gang warfare and was soon tapped by other LAPD investigators as well as the feds for his expertise. In 1997, he was asked to join Wilshire's homicide unit. One of his trainers for the new assignment was Detective Kelly Cooper, who had worked on the initial Biggie Smalls murder investigation. Before his orientation was finished, Daryn had pumped the veteran dry of every last detail pertaining to the stalled case. It was during this time that Daryn and I became close friends. It didn't hurt that he was a walking encyclopedia of information about the people I had been trying, for going on ten years, to take off the streets.

It was shortly afterward, in early 2003, that federal agents again contacted me, looking for my help to build a case against a major Los Angeles crime figure. His name was George Torres, and I had first become aware of his vast underworld enterprise during my rookie year at the Newton Division. My senior training officer there had been Detective Joannie McNamara, and during our first week together she had driven me deep into the Southside to view firsthand the headquarters of a man who was the target of a investigation she had been involved in for years. There, at the intersection of San Pedro Street and Jefferson Boulevard, was an immaculately maintained grocery store, painted a distinctive sea foam green and called Numero Uno. From its upstairs offices Torres ran a multi-faceted operation that reached from the meanest streets of the city to its highest echelons of political power.

A semiliterate Mexican immigrant, Torres had transformed a single food cart in South L.A. into an extensive chain of Numero Uno supermarkets. In the process he came to embody the immigrant dream, carefully cultivating a reputation as a committed community leader and becoming one of the largest private landowners in the region. Rubbing elbows with many of L.A.'s civic elite, he would fly a private jet out to Las Vegas for gambling excursions and lavished his seven children with expensive cars, clothes, and educations.

But authorities came to suspect that there was another side to the spectacular rise of the Southside grocery king. As early as the mid-eighties, DEA probes uncovered what they believed to be links between Torres and the Arellano-Felix drug cartel operating out of Tijuana. At the same time, LAPD homicide investigators had begun gathering evidence that suggested Torres' involvement in a number of unsolved murders throughout the area. There were also persistent rumors that he was supplying more than tortillas and chili peppers to the neighborhood. Agents looked closely at evidence suggesting that Torres oversaw a drug network employing up to thirty street dealers and mules at any one time. A federal criminal probe of George Torres was launched, centered near the Mexican border in San Diego. It was there that detectives established what they believed to be additional criminal links, this time between Torres and the infamous Reynoso Brothers International food distribution network, later to become the focus of a major Mexican drug cartel prosecution.

But the feds weren't alone in their pursuit of Torres. From almost the beginning of her tenure at Newton Division, Joannie McNamara had developed her own leads pointing to ongoing cooperation between Torres and several black gangs in the area, including the Rolling 20's Outlaw Bloods and the Five-Trey Avalon Crips, as well as such Hispanic crews as the Ghetto Boys and the Playboys. Joannie's knowledge of Torres and his operations became so extensive that she would subsequently be loaned out to help in the San Diego investigation. As she continued her intensive work, an informant claimed that there was a contract out on her life, supposedly initiated by Torres himself. When LAPD brass got wind of it, McNamara was suddenly pulled off the case and transferred, over her strong objections, to a safer posting in the San Fernando Valley. Not long afterward, the federal probe stalled and the Torres investigation was put on the shelf.

In many ways, I was carrying on the work that Joannie had begun when, in 1997, I too became caught up in the George Torres case. I helped gather information, develop informants, and interview witnesses in a variety of investigations that had picked up where the initial San Diego-based probe had left off. In cooperation with Jim Black, an ATF agent and close friend, I was able to secure funding and manpower for a dedicated task force and Operation Robin Hood—a bad police pun, playing off "robbin' the hood,"—was launched, with Black and myself at the helm.

Over the course of the next two years, although we did a lot of good work, results remained frustratingly out of reach. Evidence solid enough to take to the U.S. attorney for prosecution continued to elude us and, as with its predecessor, the steam slowly went out of the investigation. In late 1999, I was promoted to detective and transferred back to the Wilshire Division.

It's a little-understood fact of police work that initiative and motivation most often originate from the bottom up. The cops who work day in and day out on the front lines are the first to understand who the bad guys really are and how to best bring them down. When those who have worked longest and hardest on a case are transferred or reassigned, the momentum will usually dissipate. They take with them all the painstaking accumulation of evidence, criminal links, witness testimony, and the myriad other details that go into a successful investigation. It can, of course, be intensely frustrating for the officer involved, yet it's also true that a cop who has committed to catching a bad guy never forgets what he's learned.

In 2003, I had the opportunity to again focus my attention on Torres when I was asked to join yet another probe into his activities. It was to be the largest investigation yet, a sprawling multiagency effort involving the FBI, the ATF, the DEA, the LAPD, the Sheriff's Department, and various local jurisdictions. Dubbed Operation Corrido, it looked into everything from conspiracy, tax evasion, and racketeering to murder and drug trafficking. My particular area of responsibility was to investigate all alleged acts of violence attributed, directly or indirectly, to Torres.

There was no shortage of leads to follow. As I started to bear down on the new evidence that had come to light since I last worked the case, I detected what I believed to be a widespread pattern of extortion, directly related to Numero Uno's strict policy of prosecuting shoplifters to the fullest extent of the law; a law laid down by El Diablo, as Torres was commonly known. Word on the street had it that anyone caught stealing from one of his stores was taken into a back room by security guards and made to pay ten times the amount of the purloined item. If a thief needed additional persuading, the persistent rumors maintained, he would be handcuffed to scaffolding or locked in a freezer. The proceeds were then carefully recorded in ledgers and a Polaroid of the chastened and, in many cases, battered shoplifter was taken and meticulously filed.

Any merchant, of course, has the right to protect himself against thievery and even to keep an account of those who have stolen from him. But if what I was hearing was true, Torres would have been taking that principle to the extreme, in effect running his own private enforcement operation, terrorizing those he caught and making a tidy profit in the process. Further evidence of these activities was procured with a wiretap, over which we heard Torres speak directly to an associate about one of the shoplifter shakedowns. The next step was to request a search warrant of various Numero Uno outlets.

The search warrant naturally required a written application to be submitted to a judge. Preparing such a document is an exacting job, requiring well-honed language skills to put on paper the justification for violating a person's right to privacy in the pursuit of justice. Any officer worth his badge knows that every word he uses to make his case will be scrutinized, if not by a judge, then certainly by a defense attorney.

The warrant request was granted and we raided nine Numero Uno markets, coming away with more than a thousand Polaroid portraits and numerous ledgers enumerating the sums exacted from each victim. On that basis the U.S. attorney was able to put forward a case of extortion and false imprisonment against Torres, one of fifty-nine counts that eventually made it to a grand jury, including three counts of solicitation of murder, in an indictment handed down in February 2005. At that point my work in Operation Corrido was essentially done. I was free to accept the offer to help reopen the Biggie Smalls murder investigation.

CHAPTER 5

The Conspiracy

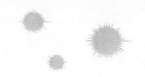

WHEN I RECEIVED THE CALL from Detective Brian Tyndall, I was under no illusion that my superiors had had a sudden attack of steely determination to bring Biggie's killer or killers to justice, no matter what it took, once and for all.

The simple fact was that the department was desperately trying to cover its ass. I knew it. Tyndall knew it. And so did everyone else who had managed to keep up with the convoluted twists and turns of the case from the beginning. There were a lot of them. It's hardly surprising that such a high-profile slaying, played out under the spotlight of celebrity, would have attracted more than its fair share of amateur sleuths and conspiracy theorists. It's especially true considering that the case had for so long been stalled, with no plausible answers forthcoming.

The Biggie Smalls murder was one of those rare events in criminal history when, in the vacuum created by the lack of closure, everything, no matter how far-fetched, seems somehow possible. When the truth is missing in action, anything can take its place. Biggie's killing was collateral damage in the long-running war between the Crips and Bloods; it was payback for Tupac Shakur's bloody demise in Las Vegas; it was an object lesson from the Nation of Islam to the runaway rap world: before it was over, all that would be missing was space aliens, the CIA, or a Biggie-Is-Alive rumor going viral in cyberspace.

But it was an LAPD detective named Russell Poole who had put forward what was, by far, the most compelling and convincing theory of what really happened and why. It was simple and elegant and fit the agendas of many of the factions that saw the death of Biggie Smalls through the lens of racism, class warfare, and the long-standing mistrust of the entrenched powers that ran Los Angeles. Simply put: the cops did it.

In every important way, Poole was a quintessential police officer, which gave his allegations of a conspiracy within the force a convincing ring of truth. For many involved in the case, he became the ultimate whistleblower, an insider with the courage to bring down the organization to which he had dedicated his professional life.

The son of a veteran L.A. County sheriff, Poole began his law enforcement career in 1981, rising quickly through the ranks to make detective in 1987 and detective supervisor in 1996. He would work as a homicide investigator at South Bureau, Wilshire, and the Robbery-Homicide Division for over nine years and was the primary detective on hundreds of cases. He helped to solve the 1997 murder of Ennis Cosby, son of comedian Bill Cosby, and was a part of the team that investigated the bloody North Hollywood bank robbery shootout that same year. Highly respected and much decorated, Poole was a cop's cop, a consummately professional officer with tireless dedication and a firm belief in his own capabilities.

Poole's role in the Biggie Smalls case began nine days after the death of Christopher Wallace in a context completely unrelated to the murder itself. He and his partner, Fred Miller, had been assigned to the homicide investigation of LAPD officer Kevin Gaines. Gaines, who had a history of aggressive behavior, had been killed when he instigated a road rage incident with another cop, an undercover detective named Frank Lyga. The cop-on-cop incident had a complicating racial element to it: Gaines was black and Lyga was white. There were some within the force, mostly friends and former partners of Gaines, who had immediately accepted the racial motivation and launched their own unofficial investigation to prove it. But for Poole, the significance of the case reached far deeper.

Early on in his probe, Poole discovered that Gaines had a girlfriend named Sharitha Knight, the estranged wife of the Death Row Records founder, Suge Knight. Following his instincts, Poole began to look closely at the dead officer's background, discovering among other intriguing details that Gaines favored expensive suits, drove a Mercedes, and frequented Monty's Steakhouse, a Westwood restaurant known as a Death Row hangout.

It was at that point that Poole felt he had "something different from your ordinary investigation…" What that "something" would turn out to be was an elaborate triangulation of rap, gangs, and corrupt cops, leading Poole to believe that Gaines had direct links to Death Row criminal activities. "He crossed the line," he would later assert in a 2001 interview with *Frontline*. "He tarnished the badge." And Gaines wasn't the only one to eventually be implicated in Poole's comprehensive conspiracy theory.

A month after the Biggie killing, the investigation—which up to then had been handled by Wilshire detectives—was handed over to the Robbery-Homicide Division. Russell Poole was named as one of the two lead detectives. From that point on, Poole assiduously worked to uncover any connection he could that might link the two investigations.

For all the lack of solid evidence or suspects, a theory of sorts had taken shape by the time Poole came aboard. As an early progress report stated, "The investigation has revealed the possibility of an ongoing feud between the victim's recording company (Bad Boy Entertainment) and Death Row Records owned by Marion (Suge) Knight. The feud is fueled by the fact that Death Row is made up of Blood gang members and that Bad Boy is comprised of Crips..."

That wasn't entirely true. Puffy's supposed use of Crips as security for concert appearances on the west coast hardly constituted membership in the gang. But at least the outlines of a workable hypothesis were emerging, one that Poole would take to with avid interest. He had already turned his focus to Suge Knight as a result of the Gaines case. From that point on, the two investigations were inexorably linked in his mind.

That link would only become more substantial to Poole as he continued to delve into the circumstances of Biggie's killing, persuading himself that the drive-by outside the Petersen was a sophisticated operation far beyond the capabilities of local gangsters to plan and execute.

"Since starting on the Biggie Smalls case," he would later tell Randall Sullivan in *LAbyrinth*, a 2002 book recounting Poole's theory of the murder, "I had kept coming across these crime reports in which the perpetrators used police radios and scanners...Suge Knight and his thugs had used them to monitor the cops...There were all these reports of the Death Row people using them in and around their studios in Tarzana." The reports were significant to Poole given the fact that, in the aftermath of Biggie's shooting, there was a persistent rumor that police radios had been used as part of a precision operation.

Witness reports of hearing scanner chatter outside the Petersen was not the only indication to Poole of a criminal conspiracy. There was the intriguing question, for instance, of how the shooter, alone in the black Impala a block away from the museum entrance, would have known exactly which vehicle Biggie had gotten into and what seat he occupied through the heavily tinted windows. The random gunfire from the Chevy Blazer on South Orange Avenue heard earlier in the evening could well have been a diversion to distract police and security guards from the real target. Poole's investigation was taking on a life of its own and the veteran cop was sure he was on to a major breakthrough. The dimensions of that breakthrough were about to be expanded by an order of magnitude.

In late 1997, while Poole was still actively working both the Gaines and Wallace investigations, the shocking news broke that a police officer had been arrested for a bank robbery that had netted $722,000, one of the largest heists in the city's history. His name was David Mack, a veteran officer of the Los Angeles Police Department. He and his one-time partner Rafael Perez would soon vie for the dubious distinction of being the most infamous rogue cops in America.

Following his arrest, Robbery-Homicide investigators began digging extensively into Mack's background. A search of his house turned up the Tec-9 he had used in the robbery as well as a large chunk of cash under the carpet. But when Russell Poole caught wind of what else had been uncovered, other crucial pieces of the puzzle he had painstakingly been assembling appeared to fall precisely into place.

First and foremost was Mack's black Chevy Impala, driven in the bank robbery but also—and of incalculably more significance to Poole—the same make of vehicle used in the Biggie drive-by. As if that were not enough to underscore Poole's belief that he had a major conspiracy between cops and gangsters on his hands, there was the bizarre discovery of what investigating officers described as a "shrine" to Tupac Shakur in Mack's home, an altar of posters and paraphernalia devoted to the slain rapper. Equally tantalizing was a tailored suit of bright crimson that had turned up in the outlaw cop's extensive wardrobe. Red, of course, was the Blood gang color and the outfit was nearly identical to one worn by Suge Knight. On top of that were the telling entries in the Rampart duty log, detailing a number of sick days Mack had taken just prior to Biggie's murder.

Yet another key clue for Poole had to do with the fact that David Mack was an avowed Muslim. More than one eyewitness to the Wallace murder had described the shooter as dressed in a suit and a bow tie. It was the bow tie, the same neckwear favored by Black Muslims, which added crucial weight to Poole's conjecture of an LAPD/Nation of Islam/Death Row conspiracy to kill the rapper.

That conjecture was furthered when Kevin Hackie, a former Compton School Police Department officer facing forgery charges, came forward with the claim that Kevin Gaines, David Mack, and Rafael Perez were part of Suge Knight's extended posse. Even if none of these cops turned out to be the actual killer, Poole reasoned, they would certainly know who was and had perhaps participated in coordinating the hit, possibly with assistance from the Fruit of Islam.

As he pushed further into the thickets of these intertwined investigations, Poole became increasingly convinced that he was being met with determined resistance from the LAPD brass. It was a case of the circular logic of conspiracy: if your theory is rejected, it's because the doubters are among the plotters, which in Poole's version of the conspiracy included the recently appointed chief of police himself, Bernard Parks. Poole had grown impatient with the reluctance of the department to investigate the link between David Mack and Suge Knight. Any attempt he made to move the sprawling investigation in that direction was rebuffed in no uncertain terms and he took that as a sign that the brass was stonewalling a major scandal within the department.

But there was another explanation to the official reluctance to follow Poole's leads. Before he was named to head the department, Parks had been an LAPD deputy chief whose duties included overseeing all investigations by Internal Affairs. If anything qualified as an IA matter, it was David Mack's criminal misconduct. As with any case that fell under the purview of Internal Affairs, all findings were subject to a near-complete information embargo. Nothing that

IA might discover during the course of its investigation could be revealed to other detectives, no matter how important it was to their ongoing work. It was a necessary restriction: Internal Affairs officers were charged with investigating their own and had to factor in the distinct possibility that where there was one corrupt cop, there might be others, trying to deflect or derail their work. A wall of silence was accordingly erected even as Poole persistently attempted to breach that barrier.

In a way, I can understand his frustration. I've been in his shoes, cut off from potentially valuable information to which only IA was privy. But that's the way the system works and it's something any detective has to come to terms with. What Poole saw as a concerted cover-up was instead a well-established precedent, making clear distinctions among all the various investigations in which he had become involved. Taking down David Mack was not Poole's responsibility. That responsibility belonged to the FBI, which was investigating Mack's involvement in the bank robbery. Poole's responsibility was to find out who had killed Biggie Smalls. If the cases converged, the preponderance of evidence would reveal the connection. Until such time, it was Poole's duty to stick to established protocols.

Poole didn't see it that way. In hindsight, evaluating the veteran detective's investigative work as he delved ever deeper into a remarkable string of circumstances, is not an easy task. His version of events—the means, methods, and motives of the Biggie Smalls murder—seemed to fit together perfectly. What was ultimately lacking was objectivity. He *wanted* to believe, and that desire, in my opinion, compromised his judgment.

The proof of that lapse can be seen, as the investigation proceeded, in Poole's reliance on jailhouse informants to support his case. In the spectrum of data-gathering techniques utilized by law enforcement, the stories told by anyone serving time are considered tainted by their very nature. While it's true that informants behind bars can, and often, do come up with useable information, it's always important to check and double-check what they tell you. Inmates have little to lose and much to gain if they can appear to be cooperating with authorities by passing along valuable information. Knowing this rule of thumb, Poole ignored it as his peril.

The first informant to come forward in the Biggie Smalls case, a mere three weeks after the murder, was Waymond Anderson, a former R&B singer who went by the stage name of Suave and was charged

Mug shot of jailhouse informant Waymond Anderson, whose tall tales would lead the investigation down several frustrating and futile rabbit holes before the truth behind the murder of Biggie Smalls was finally uncovered.

with first-degree murder for setting a house on fire and incinerating its resident. Awaiting trial at the L.A. County Jail's Wayside facility, Anderson stepped forward claiming to have information relevant to the Christopher Wallace case and hoping to exchange it for a lesser charge or a reduction in his sentence.

While in a holding tank at the Inmate Reception Center downtown, he told Wilshire detectives, Suge Knight, who was also being processed at the facility for a parole violation, approached him. According to Anderson, Suge induced him to use his gunrunning contacts to supply the weapons for the Biggie hit. He even told Anderson the names of the designated hit men: Knight's associate Wesley Crockett, his cousin Ricardo Crockett, and an ex-Compton police officer named Reginald Wright, Jr.

At the same time, it was revealed that Anderson had been in continuing conversation with another Wayside inmate named Michael Robinson. As if on cue, Robinson notified jailers that he, too, had information bearing directly on the Biggie case. In the pecking order of informants, Robinson, behind bars for robbery, was several credible cuts above Anderson. He had in the past provided highly reliable information and was so well thought of by law enforcement officials that, after his death years later, the FBI would step forward to pay his funeral expenses.

Robinson's story likewise eclipsed that of his fellow inmate in the sheer breadth and detail of the story he told. The Wallace murder, he related to investigators, had been the result of a contract put out by Suge Knight in retaliation for Tupac Shakur's death six months earlier. The shooter was a killer-for-hire, a member of the Fruit of Islam, the paramilitary branch of the Black Muslims, an associate of the Crips, and a close friend of a local gangster known as "Stutterbox." While the killer's true name was either "Kenny" or "Keeky," he was more commonly known as "Amir," "Ashmir," "Abraham," or something similarly Middle Eastern.

It was at that point that Poole had what he thought was the decisive piece of evidence to make his conspiracy case. The detective had paid a visit to the Montebello City Jail, where David Mack was being held for bank robbery. While there, Poole examined the visitors' log kept by the facility. Among the first names listed after Mack's arrest was Amir Muhammad.

"Amir." "Ashmir." "Abraham." Poole was convinced he had at last found a clue that linked David Mack directly to the killer of Biggie Smalls, as identified, however vaguely, by a jailhouse informant.

CHAPTER 6

Wrongful Death

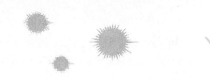

RUSSELL POOLE'S CONSPIRACY THEORY would go on to become a potent element in the perfect storm of police corruption, gang warfare, and public cynicism that descended over Los Angeles in the summer in 1998.

David Mack and his partner Rafael Perez would, of course, go on to become poster boys for the so-called Rampart Scandal, eventually involving more than seventy officers from the division, many of whom would end up being accused of everything from unprovoked shootings to planting evidence and framing suspects. Drug dealing, bank robbery, perjury, and a massive cover-up would all become part of Rampart's continuous headlines during that troubled period.

By a wide measure the most extensive case of alleged police malfeasance in U.S. history, Rampart cracked wide open in August of that year after Perez was arrested for stealing six pounds of cocaine, worth over $80,000, from an LAPD evidence room. A further inventory of the drug locker turned up another missing pound along with the bags of Bisquick that Perez had used to replace the purloined coke.

"Is this about the bank robbery?" he allegedly asked when arrested. It wasn't, nor has it ever been determined whether Perez helped Mack pull off the heist. But the inadvertent remark helped investigators tie the pair together along with several other Rampart officers. Perez would later cut a deal with prosecutors, producing four thousand pages of testimony describing a ruthless criminal subculture that had taken root at the division. Much of the account provided by Perez eventually proved to be little more than an attempt to deflect attention from his own criminal behavior onto the entire division. Of the seventy-plus officers who were implicated by Perez, fifty-eight were brought before internal administrative boards, twelve were given suspensions, seven resigned, and five were terminated. Before it was all over, the five fired officers were reinstated with full back pay.

Nevertheless, Rampart spawned nearly 150 civil lawsuits, costing the city close to $125 million in settlements. It's been suggested that Chief Bernard Parks lost his job in 2001 as a direct result of the scandal and, further, that it contributed to the defeat of Mayor James Hahn by Antonio Villaraigosa in 2005.

It was in that poisoned atmosphere that Russell Poole's assertion of cops and gangsters working the same side of the street found fertile ground. The fact that he had, at least to his own satisfaction, linked LAPD officers to Suge Knight, a high-profile gangbanger, only added fuel to the flame.

In June 1998, thanks largely to his escalating war with the LAPD, Poole was taken off the Wallace murder investigation and was eventually relieved of his duties at the Robbery-Homicide Division altogether. After being shuttled from one assignment to another over the next eighteen months, Poole resigned, devoting himself to promoting his theory, including extensive interviews for the book *LAbyrinth* and appearing in the documentary *Biggie and Tupac*, an account of his role in "breaking" the case.

In September 2000, almost a year after he had left the force, Poole filed a civil suit in federal court naming Chief Bernard Parks and the City of Los Angeles as co-defendants and alleging that the chief had violated Poole's First Amendment rights to go public with his findings. He went on to accuse the LAPD of deliberately closing off his efforts to thoroughly investigate corruption within its ranks. It was a questionable claim on the face of it, primarily because Poole had no right to "go public" with any aspect of the investigation while still a police officer. But in Poole's mind, as revealed to *LAbyrinth* author Randall Sullivan, the lawsuit was his attempt to "get the truth out the one way that was left to me."

In any event, Poole's legal maneuverings accomplished exactly the opposite. The civil suit opened the gates to a flood of legal actions and counteractions that would keep the courts busy for years, even as they further obscured whatever truth about Christopher Wallace's death might have yet been revealed.

In 2002 Biggie's mother, Voletta, his estranged wife, Faith Evans, and various members of the Wallace family filed a federal wrongful-death lawsuit, using Poole's playbook to claim an LAPD cover-up in the killing. "I'm sick to my stomach over the way this case has been handled," the aggrieved mother would later tell the *Los Angeles Times*. "There is a murderer out there laughing at my family and laughing at the cops. And it makes me furious. I've held my tongue for months now, but I'm fed up with the police just pussyfooting around."

The LAPD was quick to respond. Shortly after the family's wrongful-death suit was filed, the department launched Operation Transparency, an attempt to get out in front of whatever might be revealed in the civil case by gathering up every scrap of information existing on the Biggie Smalls investigation. Internal Affairs swept into the Robbery-Homicide headquarters and hoovered up virtually everything in sight that might conceivably have a connection to the case: police reports, detective field notes, witness interviews, forensic findings: the data filled a whopping ninety-two-volume "murder book" of four-inch thick three-ring binders. It was all hauled away and promptly sequestered, which brought the murder investigation itself to a screeching halt.

But nothing could slow down the courtroom circus into which the civil case would, over the next three years, devolve. For example, it was during the discovery process that the family's defense team became aware of a cassette recovered from the desk drawer of Detective Steven Katz, confiscated during Operation Transparency. On it, Katz was heard interviewing a jailhouse informant who confirmed that Rafael Perez had worked for Death Row Records and that, further, on the night of the murder he had placed a call to David Mack. The revelation caused an uproar, especially after Katz testified that he had simply "forgotten" about the tape's existence. "The day before this trial began," read a statement by the Wallace family in 2005, "we held a press conference and made clear that this trial was intended to hold the LAPD accountable… little did we know at the time what dark secrets lurked in the desk drawers of homicide detectives and little did we suspect that so many lies would be told under penalty of perjury."

Presiding over the trial was U.S. District Judge Florence-Marie Cooper, who seemed to agree that dark secrets were indeed lurking. She called Katz's claim of forgetfulness "utterly unbelievable" and "very disturbing." The beleaguered detective was promptly removed from the case, but the judge was far from placated. In a scathing statement just before declaring a mistrial, Cooper went on to assert, "The detective, acting alone or in concert with others, made a decision to conceal from the plaintiffs in this case information that could have supported their contention that David Mack was responsible for the Wallace murder." To underscore her displeasure, she ordered the LAPD to pay all legal fees associated with the case, as well as imposing a stiff penalty on the department. The total damages came to more than a million dollars.

But that was hardly the worst news that the city and its increasingly discredited police department would be handed in the 2002 civil judgment. In additional remarks relating to her findings, Judge Cooper let it be known that, if she were to make a ruling then and there, it would be for the plaintiffs to the tune of $500 million. The figure represented the earnings the estate claimed had been lost by Biggie's death, based on an estimate provided by the Recording Industry Association of America.

The legal maneuverings would drag on and on. Poole's First Amendment case continued to wind its labyrinthine way through the courts to no conclusive end. The Wallace family would go on to file an amended suit against the city, once again alleging a police conspiracy in the shooting and this time asserting that the LAPD had "consciously concealed Rafael Perez's involvement in the murder." In the estimation of one legal analyst hired by the city, the claims being made by the family, and the evidence being offered to support them, were not particularly compelling. The danger for the LAPD, however, was that together they would amount to "death by a thousand cuts" in the minds of the jury.

The essential weakness of the Wallace civil suit was underscored when another U.S. district judge summarily dismissed it. But five months later Judge Cooper was back with a reinstatement. What would be called by the *Los Angeles Times* "one of the longest running and most contentious cases of celebrity justice" on record had taken on a life of it's own, feeding rampant and increasingly bizarre speculation and unfounded conspiracy theories that further obscured, if that were possible, the tragedy at the heart of the case.

All those zeros in 500,000,000 had, of course, gotten the LAPD's undivided attention. There was a very real possibility that the suit would end up being among the most expensive the department had ever had to pay out. So it came as no surprise that the brass wasted no time in putting together a task force to finally solve the nine-year-old case, find the killer, and hopefully exonerate the police in the process.

I was more than ready to take on the job. The three-year-long George Torres investigation had pretty much wrapped up by then and I had gotten a taste for complex, multifaceted, and high-profile detective work. The specter of a potentially immense judgment made the resurrected investigation that much more of a priority for the department, which meant substantially more manpower and resources would be made available to the task force. I also knew that if we succeeded where others had gone off the rails, it would be a career milestone.

I would be bringing the sum of my experience and expertise as an investigating officer to the case, particularly as it applied to the intelligence I had been gathering on Los Angeles gangs for going on twenty years. I knew the turf, the players, and the feuds igniting the bloody street wars that had terrorized the city for so long. But it didn't take an expert to realize that the Biggie murder was, one way or another, gang-related.

At the same time I was only too aware that the investigation was considered by many to be cursed. There was, first and foremost, Russell Poole's ruined law enforcement career to consider. But it was the entire Robbery-Homicide Division that had taken the biggest hit to its reputation and prestige. The detectives who worked there had long considered themselves an elite unit, and it was hard to swallow the embarrassment of allowing such a significant investigation to go completely cold. The simple truth was that there were no volunteers stepping forward from RHD to join the fledgling task force. It was more than a little unusual to put together an investigative team on a major murder case *not* made up of the Robbery-Homicide detectives, but it also worked to our advantage. A central pivot of the investigation was, after all, the possibility of police involvement. RHD had conspicuously failed to find the killer. Was that a result of plain bad luck, uncharacteristic incompetence, or a department-wide cover-up? To find the answer to that question, it made better sense to draw in recruits from across the board and allow them to follow leads that could possibly take them to Robbery-Homicide's downtown headquarters.

Which, in itself, led to the inevitable question.

"Brian," I asked straight up when Tyndall called me on May 1, 2006, with his offer to join the team, "are we supposed to solve this case or are we supposed to protect the department?"

"Greg," he replied, "we're going to go wherever this takes us. You have my word on it."

That meant a lot. A free hand to do the job was my one non-negotiable stipulation, even if it meant exposing an LAPD conspiracy or cover-up. That was especially true since, up to that point, I had been on the outside of the case. Like a lot of people, I was inclined to believe at least some of Poole's conjectures. The inescapable conclusion was that among my fellow officers were the very suspects we would be searching out.

I also knew that Tyndall wouldn't be telling me just what I wanted to hear. He was too good a cop, and we'd known each other for too long, for evasion to be a factor. I'd first met Brian Tyndall back in 1994 when he was part of an Officer Involved Shooting Squad along with Bill Holcomb, another initial member of the evolving Biggie Smalls task force. I came before them after an incident when, observing a street fight on patrol, I had pursued one of the combatants into a nearby house. When he pulled a gun I shot him with what was my own version of a "magic bullet." Purely as a result of the angle of the trajectory, one slug made a grand total of five holes and deprived him of his testicles in the process.

Tyndall and Holcomb's investigation resulted in a finding that the incident had been "in policy." Brian had afterward gone on to distinguish himself as an outstanding officer, especially with his work on the David Mack bank robbery and the wider Rampart Scandal.

He had, in fact, partnered with Russell Poole on various aspects of the case and had come out on record as saying that allegations of involvement by Rampart officers in the Wallace killing might well be true.

Tyndall was friendly and easygoing, with a perpetually positive attitude and the kind of seasoned outlook that accommodated an ability to stay above the fray. Part of that relaxed disposition probably had to do with the fact that, at the point when he took over the helm of the task force, he had been technically retired. One of the most lucrative perks available to a career policeman is called DROP (Deferred Retirement Option Program), which allows any officer of retirement age to stay on the job an additional five years at full salary while still collecting a pension. Tyndall was, in effect, being paid twice for doing the same job he'd always done. Small wonder he had a tolerant outlook on the sometimes tedious routines of police work. I wouldn't say he lacked motivation: far from it. He was too professional for that. But whatever was going to happen or not happen in the new Biggie Smalls probe, Tyndall could well afford to take it all in stride.

The same could be said for Detective Bill Holcomb, another DROP beneficiary. While it's easy to imagine Tyndall and Holcomb as complacent timeservers, content to sit out their delayed retirement while socking away piles of cash, that wasn't really the case. Once the real work of the task force got under way, they both proved adept at running interference between the team's more hands-on investigators and the LAPD administrators who were keeping a nervous eye on our progress. They were, in the truest sense of the term, "user-friendly" supervisors who made sure we had the freedom to pursue any and all leads while making the appropriate soothing sounds to placate the brass.

It was a job that, under the circumstances, required considerable diplomacy. Concurrent with the task force investigation, Internal Affairs was also continuing the probe into a possible police conspiracy. Both supervisors were required to provide IA with any and all information we might uncover relating directly to David Mack, Rafael Perez, and anyone else with connections, real or imagined, to Death Row and Suge Knight. At the same time, they also had to be careful to insure that whatever they shared would not result in our own efforts being shut down or taken over directly by IA. Navigating these conflicting interests required savvy political skills.

But from the onset there was another, more formidable hurdle to overcome: there was nothing to investigate. During Operation Transparency, Internal Affairs had carted off every last scrap of information and evidence related to the investigation and was keeping it under lock and key. Notwithstanding the city's frantic demand that the case be solved immediately if not sooner, IA hung on to the murder books, leaving the task force nothing to work with. Short of starting the entire investigation again from scratch, the team had little choice but to wait patiently for IA to laboriously copy the reams of documents and return them in a slow and frustrating trickle. As the photocopies slowly piled up, Tyndall and Holcomb realized that it would take a herculean effort just to bring order to the case, never mind trying to actually move it forward. It was at that point that Tyndall began to expand the task force. I was his first call.

My answer was immediately and enthusiastically affirmative. The reason was simple: I wanted to solve the case. I wanted to solve it very badly. Of course, I also wanted to see justice done. I wanted the family, after so long, to finally know for sure who had killed Christopher Wallace and why. But what really motivated me was the chance to succeed where so many others had failed, to make the case my own.

CHAPTER 7

The Team

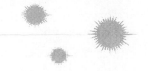

IN MOVIES AND ON TV, a team comes together when a mastermind assembles his specialized crew—the munitions expert, the computer geek, the muscleman, the femme fatale—to take on an impossible mission. In real life, it doesn't exactly work that way. When Tyndall and Holcomb were charged with forming the Biggie Smalls task force, they had to balance many conflicting interests, only one of which was actually solving the case.

In putting together a law enforcement task force, one of the first general considerations is whether or not the target is "viable." Viability usually means the likelihood of seizing assets that will help to offset the cost of funding the team itself. It's an expensive proposition, usually far beyond the budgets of most police departments, to support an effective task force. Overtime, travel expenses and informant payments are only part of the bottom line. One of the most valuable tools in such investigations, for example, is a wiretap, which requires considerable outlay, first to the phone company for the installation of the eavesdropping equipment, then for the monitors hired to actually listen to and transcribe the conversations, hour after hour, day after day. Getting a task force off the ground means convincing the brass of a reasonable return on such investments.

In that regard, the revamped Biggie Smalls investigation had an advantage going in. Aside from our primary goal of bringing the killer or killers to justice, our success in solving the case would potentially be saving the department $500 million, the amount Judge Cooper had held out as a possible settlement for the Wallace family wrongful-death suit. Securing money and manpower was not going to be a major problem for us.

When a local task force is faced with funding restraints, the way the job usually gets done is by expanding the scope of the investigation. Bringing in other agencies can help to defray the costs and provide access to resources that would not normally be available. One of the first moves I made after answering Tyndall's call was to push for the same kind of multi-pronged approach, but for very different reasons. It was immediately clear to me that the job was simply too big for the LAPD to handle by itself. We needed the best experts, the latest technology, and a long legal reach. There was only one place to go to get all that: the feds.

Federalizing the investigation made sense on a lot of levels, and accordingly, I approached Timothy Searight, assistant U.S. attorney for California's Central District, with my proposal. I had worked with Searight on a couple of previous cases, most notably the Torres investigation, and knew him to be a smart and capable prosecutor. He immediately saw the potential in the approach I was pushing for and agreed to assist in deputizing the team as agents of the federal government. As a result, Searight would oversee the procedural aspects of the investigation, which would also be to our advantage, thanks to an important difference between federal and local prosecutorial methods. As an LAPD officer, my responsibility would have been to gather up enough evidence for a district attorney to decide whether the case was strong enough to go to trial. In the federal system, a U.S. attorney works with the investigators from the inception of a case, supervising its progress at each stage to maximize the potential for a successful prosecution. Searight, in short, would become a de facto member of the team.

With the lingering cloud of police involvement still hanging over the Biggie killing, having the presence of outside agencies on the team meant that it would be a lot harder for anyone to claim that we were just a tool of the LAPD, attempting to provide cover for its culpability.

At the same time we would benefit from the enhanced authority that a federalized task force would automatically wield. Being deputized allowed us to utilize a whole range of enforcement tools not normally within our jurisdiction, including the significantly enhanced sentencing guidelines that would come with a conviction in any federal court. If we were going to find the killer and any co-conspirators, a trial in federal court would ensure a punishment that fit the crime.

This was a key consideration in light of the stalled nature of the case itself. After nine years, the likelihood that we were going to uncover some revelatory new clue or turn up a witness who hadn't already been interviewed a dozen times was pretty slim. The investigation had exhausted itself a long time ago and it was going to take some extraordinary incentives to pry new information from those who had told their story, stuck to it all along, and would have no good reason to cooperate with us this time around. Without the ability to exert new and serious pressure, all we would be doing was listening to the same shopworn tales one more time.

Opening the case up as a federal investigation would give us that leverage. With the resources and enforcement muscle of the FBI, the ATF, the DEA, and other federal agencies behind us, we could bring to bear all sorts of new legal incentives. The most compelling was the distinct possibility of Racketeer Influenced and Corrupt Organizations (RICO) indictments, which provided stringent penalties for acts performed as part of an ongoing criminal organization, up to and including twenty years on each and every racketeering count.

The logic was unassailable. Any investigation into the death of Biggie Smalls would have to immediately come to terms with the reality of the Bloods and Crips war that had been raging for close to a decade and would almost certainly be a factor in the murder. For example, the link between the Mob Piru Bloods subset of the Bloods and Suge Knight's Death Row Records would be the logical place to start looking. If anyone within Death Row knew who killed Biggie and why, the threat of a RICO conviction might be all that was needed to get a target talking. We might finally be able to break the logjam that had blocked the case for so long.

Of course, focusing on Crips and Bloods as continuous criminal enterprises was hardly a new idea. Nor was the connection between gangs and rap record companies. "Rap music organizations were created with profits from existing criminal drug enterprises," Bill Holcomb stated bluntly in an early task force memo. And while it was true that not all rap labels had criminal ties, Holcomb's statement mirrored the widespread perception at the time regarding rap's gangster connections.

The criminal links to rap reached back almost to the inception of black Los Angeles gangs themselves, a history that began in the mid-sixties when the original Crips were first formed. By the end of the decade, they ruled the streets of South Central L.A. until, in 1972, another group, centered on Piru Street in Compton, formed their own crew. To differentiate themselves from their rivals, who dressed in blue, the upstarts wore red, borrowed from the colors of Centennial High School, which many of them attended. They called themselves Bloods or, interchangeably, Pirus. There were eventually more than fifty separate and distinct subsets of the two gangs, funded primarily through the sale of marijuana and PCP, as well as robberies, burglaries, and auto thefts.

The late seventies experienced a terrifying escalation in gang power, fueled by the insidious rise of crack cocaine, which ushered in a new era of well regimented drug distribution networks. These criminal enterprises were overseen by the "O.G.s", the original gangsters who had first formed the gangs. "Ballers" bought the rock cocaine and distributed it to a descending order of street peddlers, beginning with the "B.G.s" (Baby Gangsters) and on down to the "T.G.s" (Tiny Gangsters.)

The plague of smokable, instantly addictive cocaine was a financial windfall of unprecedented dimensions in modern criminal history. At the same time, the reach of the Crips and Bloods radiated steadily outward from South Central L.A., as they established chapters across the country, ruthlessly eliminating local competition in the drug trade. The enormous profits swelling gang coffers gave rise to what would become known as the "gangster lifestyle," which would find its most popular expression in gangsta rap. Street-corner MCs celebrated in rhythm and rhyme their gangster heroes and were, in turn, provided with recording budgets paid for with drug proceeds. This close association between music and mobsters began with such gangster rap pioneers as Eric "Easy E" Wright, a known affiliate of the Atlantic Drive and the Kelly Park Crips. "Easy E's" groundbreaking company Ruthless Records had been directly financed by drug cash, a fact widely attested to even on the rapper's posthumous Facebook posting, as well by such music industry journalists as David N. Howard in his book *Sonic Alchemy.*

By the early nineties, rap music had become far and away the most popular form of music in the world. Gangster rap was its most potent variant, a myth-making music that often chronicled the bloody rivalry between Crips and Bloods.

Given that rivalry, and the part it almost certainly played in the murder we were investigating, I advised Tyndall and Holcomb to split the focus of the task force, gathering information on the Crips into a case file dubbed "*Menace II Society*," while anything having to do with Mob Piru became part of another file called "*Rap It Up*." It was a way to bring order and manageability to an already complicated case.

But the complications were just beginning. The most daunting task we faced in the first days was picking the right personnel. In the process, we came up hard against a long-established view within the LAPD that detectives are more or less interchangeable. It was an attitude I encountered early in my tenure with the Robbery-Homicide Division, when I heard a commander say that, in his opinion, any detective should be able to take over a case from any other detective at a moment's notice. I wondered at the time what, if that were true, was the point of developing specific areas of crime-fighting expertise, but I'd long since given up expecting an answer.

In fact, my first priority after joining the task force was to proactively gather officers with the specialized knowledge and experience that the investigation would require. My first candidate was Daryn Dupree. After his stint at the Wilshire Division, first in the CRASH unit and then as a homicide investigator, Daryn had been transferred to West Bureau Gangs in recognition of his extraordinary expertise in many aspects of Los Angeles gang activity. While gang involvement was virtually a given in the Biggie shooting, what was even more telling was that the killing had occurred at the interface of street gangs and the rap music business. Daryn had a deep knowledge of how and where these realms overlapped and of the complex gangster influence on the rap industry and vice versa. Of course, it didn't hurt that he was also a close friend. Even though his superiors, in light of his track record, were reluctant to let him go, Daryn quickly became the newest member of the task force.

Another selection was Alan Hunter, who seemed like a logical choice, primarily because he had considerable gang experience, as both a member of the Wilshire CRASH unit and a detective in RHD.

Quiet and outwardly unassuming, Hunter was in fact a tightly wound officer with a low threshold for aggressive behavior. A competent if not exactly creative detective, Alan had trouble thinking outside the box, and if there was one thing the Biggie Smalls case needed, it was innovative approaches to the formidable challenges we faced. In contrast, Alan's investigative technique was tethered to a textbook application of routine police work. Moreover, in a job that required all the cooperating witnesses we could get, Alan's in-your-face interrogation techniques would serve to alienate some of the same people we were trying to win over.

Other choices, however, would quickly prove their merit. Deputy Tim Brennan of the Los Angeles Sheriff's Department was a former Compton cop, known throughout the 'hood as "Blondie." Brennan had made it his business to become the unofficial historian of the city's streets and had a wealth of specialized knowledge regarding Southside Crips and Blood gangs. Unfortunately, it came at a price. There was a trace of apprehension toward Blondie among the other task force members due to his links with a small core of ex-Compton cops who had gone on to work security for Death Row Records.

It was an apprehension that reached deep into the wider ranks of the LAPD. Because it was outside city limits, Compton was not within the department's jurisdiction. Being part of the county, it fell instead under the County Sheriff's purview. From the time it was first incorporated in 1888, the feisty municipality had opted to oversee its own law enforcement, appointing a city marshal to circumvent county control. A century later, the reputation of the Compton Police Department was among the most tarnished in the nation. It was for that reason, among others, that the city council disbanded it in 2000 and turned policing authority over to the Sheriff's Department.

The stench of that corruption inevitably clung to anyone who had served time in the Compton police department. Given our increasing belief in gang involvement in the Biggie homicide, such qualms were understandable, but it only meant Brennan would work that much harder to allay our suspicions and render valuable service to the team. On both counts he performed admirably.

Three more recruits would eventually join the task force, the first being an LAPD investigator named Frank Trujillo whose background with Internal Affairs provided an important liaison function with a department that was running its own probe into many of the same areas where we were venturing. Another LAPD officer, named Omar Bazulto, who would soon show his mettle as an analyst and field agent, also came aboard. So, too, did a series of agents assigned to us by the FBI as part of our multi-agency task force, eventually including Jeff Bennett, whose usefulness was hampered by his limited experience. He had been with the Bureau for only two years prior to joining us.

Within a few days of receiving the call from Tyndall, I joined the rest of the team for an initial debriefing and orientation. It was only then that I began to realize the magnitude of the job with which we'd been tasked. The volumes of evidentiary material that Internal Affairs had confiscated as part of Operation Transparency had only just been returned, and the material was in a state of complete disorganization. Within those tens of thousands of random pages were scores of witness interviews, reams of field reports, and piles of often-indecipherable handwritten detective notes, running down every theory and conjecture relating to the murder, no matter how absurd or incidental, from the first moments of the shooting to the point where the whole case collapsed under its own weight.

As if all that were not enough to deal with, we were also bequeathed with, thanks to our newly federalized status, the results of an exhaustive FBI investigation into the racketeering activities of Death Row Records that had lasted from 1995 to 2001. The probe had been thwarted by the events of September 11, which, of course, required an extensive reallocation of the Bureau's resources and manpower.

But the massive evidence files still existed on the FBI database and were accordingly dumped in our laps.

Before we could even begin the job of sorting through the ruins of the case, we needed a place to work. We headed to the basement supply room to pick up the desks, chairs, computers, and filing cabinets we would need to furnish the offices that had been assigned to us in the headquarters of the Robbery-Homicide Division. So sensitive was the brass to the integrity of the investigation that we were each given a key to the room along with strict orders that no one was to be allowed to enter without our express knowledge and permission. We subsequently acquired workspace at the DEA office as well, a mile away in downtown Los Angeles.

Over the course of the first month, Daryn and I took the lead in reorganizing the murder books, in the process constructing an extensive flow chart replete with the name, affiliation, and, where possible, photo of every witness, suspect, bystander, and tangential player that figured, however marginally, into the case. Lines of association connected each and the chart was color-coded for easy reference. The result occupied an entire wall in the task force office and became a primary tool for the team as the investigation moved forward.

As we began to slowly absorb the sprawling scope of what we were facing, it became increasingly apparent there were elements of the case that would require an entirely new kind of investigative approach. The challenge wasn't simply in the time that had elapsed since the killing, the witnesses who had since died, or the key evidence that had vanished. It wasn't even the fact that the killer or killers had had nine years to cover their tracks. What really made the case unique was that it had been pushed far past hard evidence and quantifiable facts and into the realm of rampant rumor and speculation. Biggie's murder was freighted with different meanings to different people: police conspiracy; rap war revenge; gang retaliation. Over the course of nearly a decade, all those different interpretations had undergone steady expansion and elaboration. The task force that had assembled under that wall-sized flow chart didn't have to just solve a murder case. It had to unravel dozens of versions of the same event, each with its own means, motive, and opportunity. Closing the case would require teasing out the truth from all the baggage it had accumulated.

The only way to do that, I concluded, would be to conduct the investigation from the outside *in*. We would tackle every theory, no matter how harebrained, treating it as real until it could be proven otherwise and disposing of them one by one until eventually we arrived at the one that could not be disproved or discredited. That, by the process of elimination, would be the truth.

Los Angeles Police Department Detective Daryn Dupree, whose outstanding work was instrumental in solving the murders of Biggie Smalls and Tupac Shakur.

Murder Rap author and former Los Angeles Police Department Detective Greg Kading.

PART
THREE

CHAPTER 8

Clearing The Rubble

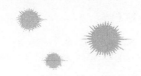

FROM THE MOMENT WE OPENED for business in May 2006 the team made it our first order of business to deal with some of the raft of rumors and unanswered questions that had dogged the investigation from the beginning.

The first one we tackled was the belief that the 1995 white Toyota Land Cruiser, seen on Fairfax Avenue on the night of the shooting, was part of a wider criminal conspiracy. The conjecture was that the vehicle, which had made an abrupt U-turn on the four-lane street and tried to wedge itself between the back up cars in Biggie's caravan, was proof that the hit was the result of a well-executed operation involving multiple plotters. The Toyota had deliberately attempted to cut off the follow-up SUVs, the theory went, preventing the bodyguards from rushing to Wallace's aid. Much was made of its sudden and mysterious appearance, not to mention its abrupt and complete disappearance.

But the real story was much simpler and not without an element of absurdity. In the white Land Cruiser that night were the two hapless hangers-on Scott Shepherd, who had come to California hoping to promote Biggie's birthday as a gala entertainment event, and his pal, the screenwriter Ernest "Troia" Anderson, who wanted to write a biopic of the rapper's life. On the night of the murder, Shepherd and Anderson had tagged along behind the entourage from the Westwood Marquee to the Vibe party. In the ensuing chaos outside the Petersen, Shepherd had tried to shoehorn his way back into the departing convoy in the hope of eventually cornering Biggie with his proposal at the evening's next stop, the after-after-party hosted by a record executive. When shots rang out, the frightened pair took off at top speed.

Troia was nothing if not persistent. Years later his number would frequently pop up on Suge Knight's phone records. It seems that Anderson was now interested in the life story of the gangster music mogul.

As with the white Land Cruiser, the mysterious black Bronco seen on South Orange Grove Avenue just after midnight was likewise easily explained. More than one eyewitness had reported hearing a single shot being fired from the vehicle, and ever since, speculation had revolved around a diversionary tactic designed to distract attention from the main target.

The reality was considerably more mundane, if not downright laughable. On the night of the murder, two Wilshire Division patrol officers received a call for assistance from Fire Department personnel on the scene at the Petersen. They called in a report of the gunfire and eyewitness accounts of a male African American fleeing the scene, southbound on Orange Grove Avenue. A bystander had seen the license plate and reported it to a Fire Department official who had passed it along to the patrolmen. Subsequently, as the officers were assisting in crowd control after Biggie was shot, a black Ford Explorer—not a Bronco—with plates matching the earlier description pulled over next to them on Wilshire Boulevard.

"Who got shot?" asked the unsuspecting driver. Instead of answering, the officers immediately took him and his passenger into custody. A subsequent search of the Explorer revealed a .25-caliber semiautomatic handgun in the map pocket of the driver side door. When questioned about the weapon and the shot fired, the driver produced a bizarre, but perfectly plausible, explanation. He and his friend had arrived at the Petersen in hopes of gaining entrance to the Vibe party. As they opened the car door to make their way to the museum entrance, his firearm fell out of the map pocket and onto the street. Concerned that the weapon might be damaged, he fired it into the air to see if it still worked. Spooked by the crowd's panicked reaction, he peeled out, only to return later to see what all the excitement was about, and was promptly arrested for illegal discharge of a firearm. The officer's report had been sitting all along in the case files.

A careful study of the initial investigation revealed that, far from the accusations of ineptitude that had dogged the police from the earliest hours following the murder, there had been a lot of solid work done, most notably by Detective Kelly Cooper, the lead officer on the case and the same bluff and by-the-book veteran who had been one of Daryn's training officers in homicide. Cooper and his team had fanned out in the days following the shooting, taking statements from anyone and everyone with even the slightest tangential connection to the case. Vibe employees helping to host the party; passing motorists and the RTD bus driver on the Wilshire route; the Petersen maintenance supervisor; LAFD personnel at the scene; clerks at the various hotels where Biggie and his posse stayed; boyfriends and girlfriends and the family relations of countless individuals on the scene—virtually no one escaped their attention.

A complete investigation of Gecko ammunition, the relatively rare type of slug that killed Biggie, was launched, and the only two distributors in the country, based in California and New Jersey, were contacted. The sales brochure of a 1996 Chevy Impala SS was procured and carefully studied, while the Air Support Division was summoned to fly over a South Central location where a black Impala had been reportedly stashed. Surveillance tapes provided by Petersen security and Cedars-Sinai Medical Center were scrutinized, and detectives would fly to Texas to interview the Houston fans who had shot the jittery video from their van across Fairfax in the minutes leading up to the murder. They would also fly to Teaneck, New Jersey, to inform Voletta Wallace of the investigation's progress and, in return, would receive a visit from narcotics officers in Teaneck who had contacted LAPD to appraise them of an indictment on drug charges that was being prepared against Christopher Wallace and others. As a result, additional officers were assigned to serve as a liaison with the New Jersey investigators.

Assisting in the early stages of the case was Tim Brennan. Blondie's gang expertise would prove especially useful in the initial phase of the probe, and he was able to single out suspects worthy of special attention from investigators. Among them were such noted gang members as Orlando "Baby Lane" Anderson, Shayne Catskill, Aaron "Heron" Palmer and the Crip shot caller Duane Keith "Keffe D" Davis, all of whom had served time for a variety of offenses. It was Keffe D who had been described by at least one witness as a friend of Puffy's and had been seen talking with Biggie at the Petersen shortly before the shooting. These names would regularly appear and reappear as the investigation progressed, with Brennan's input particularly invaluable for detectives trying to tie the murder to the ongoing gang feuds in which Keffe D and the others were involved.

But, as is the case with any high-profile investigation, there was also an abundance of complete dead ends. Detectives found themselves, for example, expending valuable time and resources chasing down a random ATM card found at the crime scene that in the end proved to be nothing more than a careless loss by its owner, caught in the stampede outside the Petersen.

Tips, anonymous and otherwise, flooded in. Local and national press coverage was carefully cataloged, and the television program *America's Most Wanted* passed along a fax received by producers claiming the existence of a videotape revealing the killer's identity. A woman who gave her name only as "Barbara" called to tell police that her daughter had information relevant to the case. The Kern County Sheriff's Department contacted the task force with the news that they had someone in custody who insisted that Biggie's killer was a man named "Rodney." Shown a composite sketch of the shooter, an informant absolutely, positively indentified him as a Grape Street Crips member named "Mike." The abundance of vague hunches, wild guesses, gut feelings, and suspects known only by their first names continued unabated for months. Each one needed to be treated seriously by detectives, but it was an overwhelming task. It's a tried-and-true law of police work that the more time elapses after the crime is committed, the colder the case gets, and increasingly the investigators could feel this case slipping away from them.

Yet, in the final analysis, Cooper and his team had conducted a thorough and exhaustive investigation, one that in time would provide a strong foundation for our resurrected case. The fact that investigating officers ultimately failed to find the killer had nothing to do with incompetence or police complicity and everything to do with rampant speculation on the street and in the press. The outcry would reach a near-hysterical pitch in the weeks following the murder, producing a thick cloud of confusion and cross-purposes that hung persistently over the case. Cooper had done his best to clamp a lid on the rising tide of rumors and hearsay, immediately sequestering, among other evidence, Wallace's autopsy file. "A lot of people are naturally curious about this case," he commented in a ringing understatement. "So we placed a security hold on it so no information could get out."

It was far too late for that. But Cooper soldiered on, doggedly continuing with the essential, if often fruitless, legwork required in any homicide investigation. And, tentative as it might have been, he was beginning to make some headway. Even in those early stages, suggestions of an intriguing connection to another high-profile case were already beginning to surface. In the mandatory sixty-day Murder Investigation Progress Report, based on material gathered by Cooper and his team, officers reported receiving "several anonymous calls saying that Wallace's homicide was related to the death of Tupac Shakur." Such vague but persistent inklings would in time become an important focus of the ongoing Biggie investigation. Detectives contacted the Las Vegas Police Department, requesting to be updated on developments in the still-unsolved Shakur murder. A subsequent report, issued six months after the murder, dealt with "the possibility of an ongoing feud between the victim's recording company (Bad Boy Entertainment) and Death Row Records, owned by Marion (Suge) Knight."

It described two key incidents, one in late 1994, the other a year later. The first occurred at a New York recording studio where unknown assailants had shot and gravely wounded Tupac in an apparent robbery attempt. The other had happened in a private club in Atlanta and pitted a Death Row posse against a Bad Boy crew, resulting in the shooting death of Suge Knight's bodyguard Jake Robles. The link between these two incidents and the Biggie shooting was, at best, tenuous, but detectives were increasingly convinced that their investigation would eventually turn on the bloody feud between the gangs and their affiliated rap labels. "Detectives have conducted approximately one hundred interviews of both Crip and Blood members," the report concluded, "in hopes of obtaining information relating to this murder and other unsolved crimes."

Those hopes were thwarted when in April, a little more than a month after the murder, the case was effectively taken out of Cooper's hands and transferred downtown to the Robbery-Homicide Division, under the auspices of the lead investigator, Russell Poole, who would turn the investigation in an entirely different direction, focusing almost solely on the possibility of a police conspiracy.

The lines Poole would draw between the outlaw elements at Rampart Division and the gang activity swirling around Death Row Records would exert a powerful hold on public perception. David Mack, Rafael Perez, and a handful of other rogue cops would be linked by Poole's theory to Suge Knight's criminal enterprise, despite the fact that direct evidence of such a connection had never been established. The most common misconception is that the officers had been hired as Death Row security. It's certainly true that many police officers moonlight on a regular basis, as demonstrated by the presence of the Inglewood cop Reggie Blaylock on the Bad Boy bodyguard squad for the Soul Train celebrations. But, while different jurisdictions have different regulations concerning outside employment, no department would ever sanction an officer hiring himself out to a known criminal enterprise. Despite numerous and persistent reports to the contrary, neither Mack nor Perez nor anyone else in the LAPD, with the exception of a bit player from Newton named Richard McCauley, were ever on the Death Row payroll.

Of all the possible conjectures our task force would have to wrestle to the ground in the initial phase of the reopened investigation, those put forth by Poole were by far the most entrenched. After joining the team, I immediately picked up a copy of *LAbyrinth*, the 2002 book written by Randall Sullivan, which laid out Poole's theory in great detail. Central to that account was the mysterious Amir Muhammad, who had left his name on the visitors' log at the Montebello City Jail when he came to see David Mack. For anyone, and there were many, who accepted Poole's version of events leading up to March 9, 1997, Amir Muhammad was the key that would unlock the truth of a deep-rooted police conspiracy. But the key didn't fit and Amir turned out to be a lot less sinister than Poole had posited. He was eventually revealed to be Harry Billups, who, as an avowed Muslim, had changed his name to Amir Muhammad. Billups had a reasonable alibi for paying a call on the prisoner. He and Mack were friends, having attended the University of Oregon together, where they had been on the track and field team. Be that as it may, Poole's accusations stuck and Billups was promptly fingered as being the possible hit man at the Petersen. It didn't help that he bore a passing resemblance to the figure with the bow tie and fade haircut outside the museum, or Bad Boy bodyguard Eugene Deal would tentatively identify him as the "Nation Of Islam guy" behind the wheel of the Impala. Yet, through it all, Billups staunchly maintained his innocence. "I'm not a murderer, I'm a mortgage broker," he told the *Los Angeles Times* before the paper was forced to retract a story connecting him with the Biggie slaying.

But Billups' ordeal didn't stop there. After Poole resigned in 1999, the FBI launched a police corruption investigation targeting David Mack. In the course of the probe, agents interviewed the jailhouse informant Michael Robinson, who had revealed that Biggie's killer was named Amir or something similar. He would subsequently go on to insist that he could also positively identify the suspect. The FBI decided to find out just how accurate the informant's claim was, outfitting Robinson with a wire and sending him directly to Billups's house. The resulting encounter quickly devolved into farce as Billups answered the door to find a complete stranger trying to make small talk, all the while being monitored by FBI agents down the street. Billups summoned the cops, who arrived to arrest the intruder before they got a frantic call from the eavesdropping FBI agents, afraid of having their informant's cover blown. The police retreated even as Billups loudly insisted that he wanted to file a complaint. In light of this embarrassing incident, the viability of Harry Billups as a suspect dropped several notches in the estimation of the task force.

So, too, did the significance of the black Impala. The vehicle was, in fact, the ride of choice among many gangsters and rap moguls at that time. Among the half dozen black Impalas that would make an appearance over the course of the investigation was one belonging to Suge Knight, another driven by a bodyguard for DJ Quik, and still others owned by David Mack and Keffe D. Given this abundance of Impalas, the likelihood of finding the actual car used in the murder was, to say the least, not high. We had nothing more to go on than its color, make and year. The absence of any other distinguishing marks, along with the fact that so many Impalas were being driven by suspects and witnesses to the crime, caused us to look elsewhere for a solid lead.

By the early fall of 2006, we had pretty much cleared away enough of the debris that had piled up around the cold case to begin the actual work of a new investigation. The question was where to begin. Knocking down flimsy theories and eliminating false leads was one thing. Building a new case on reliable information was quite another. We had our work cut out for us.

CHAPTER 9

Fishing Expeditions

ONCE WE SORTED OUT where we didn't need to go, we began looking around for new ways forward in the long-stalled case. With virtually every witness wrung dry years before, we knew we had to come at the investigation from a fresh angle, identifying those who might have undisclosed information and then finding a way to pry it loose.

Fortunately for us, there were more than a few persons of interest in the case who were already in jail, awaiting trial, or serving time on a variety of unrelated charges. Maybe they could be induced to stop stonewalling and start talking, which meant that we had to have something to bargain with: like a reduced sentence, a good word in a plea bargain, or some other form of special consideration.

What we had going for us was the fact that they were almost all gang members. Gangs are tight-knit clans, with extended family relationships that afford members the favored status of "cuz" in their particular set. As a result, everyone pretty much knew what was going on with everyone else. There was a lot of talk, gangster-to-gangster, as well as the usual bragging and bagging that went on between rival sets. Word, even of the most incriminating variety, inevitably got around.

Such was the case with Trevon "Tray" Lane, who was in L.A. County Jail awaiting trial on a charge of evading police. Tim Brennan and I paid him a visit in early July. Tray was uniquely qualified to tell us something we didn't already know, given his involvement in an incident that had led up to the shooting of Tupac Shakur in Las Vegas on September 7, 1996.

Two months prior to that night, Tray, his friend Kevin "K.W." Woods, and two other Bloods had been shopping at a Foot Locker outlet in the Lakewood Mall, a sprawling shopping complex between Compton and Long Beach that was a favorite spot for gangsters to strut their stuff. That evening, Tray was sporting a large diamond-cut medallion stamped with the Death Row logo, a prized piece of bling bestowed on favored associates by Suge Knight. As the foursome left the mall and made their way through the parking lot, they were jumped by upward of eight Southside Crips, including Maurice "Lil Mo" Combs, Denvonta "Dirt" Lee, and Orlando "Baby Lane" Anderson.

Baby Lane would subsequently appear on the list of likely suspects Brennan had supplied to detectives in the initial Biggie Smalls investigation. Tall and rangy with an ice-cold stare, Baby Lane had been arrested for murder in 1996 and on a robbery charge the following year. But his rap sheet paled in comparison with the crimes he was suspected of committing but that could not be proved. They included involvement in a number of drive-by shootings and other gang-related assaults. He was the quintessential menace to society.

But Anderson had simple larceny on his mind that afternoon in the parking lot of the Lakewood Mall. Specifically, he was after the gaudy gold-and-diamond Death Row necklace that Tray was wearing.

Later stories circulated that Puffy had offered a $10,000 bounty to anyone who could bring him one of these medallions. Compton police officer Reggie Wright, Jr., had heard rumors to that effect from the Southside Crips and had passed the information along to investigators during the initial probe into Biggie's death.

But it's much more likely that Anderson simply wanted the pendant with its heavy chain for himself. And he got it, ripping it off Tray's neck and leaving the humiliated Pirus to plot their revenge.

They had their chance several weeks later when Tupac and Suge were in Las Vegas to see Mike Tyson take on the WBA heavyweight champion, Bruce Seldon, in one of the more controversial boxing matches in recent sports history. Tyson took out Seldon in the first round, knocking him down twice with blows that the slow-motion replay footage later suggested had either missed the defending champ completely or simply grazed him. The fight was called after a little less than two minutes, with cries of "Fix!" echoing through the MGM Grand Garden Arena.

But Tyson's questionable punches weren't the only ones thrown that night. Also in town for the fight was a contingent of Crips, including Baby Lane. At close to nine o'clock, following the main event, Anderson was making his way across the lobby of the MGM Grand Hotel. Tray, who had accompanied Tupac and Suge to Las Vegas, spotted him across the crowded room, leaning over to whisper in Tupac's ear.

"That's the dude," he reportedly said, identifying Anderson as the Crip who had stolen Tray's Death Row medallion and the two moved quickly across the casino floor.

"You from the South?" Tupac asked Baby Lane before laying him out on the plush carpet with a sucker punch. His posse, including Suge, piled on with kicks and blows to the face and torso in a vicious assault that, clocking in at one minute and nine seconds, lasted nearly as long as the championship bout they had just attended.

The entire incident was captured on a hotel security camera, the roving eye of the lens following an attractive woman across the lobby past an elaborate carved glass sculpture. She suddenly recoils and the camera pans over to record a flurry of blows and kicks, then tracks Tupac and his entourage hurrying across the lobby as security guards scramble to figure out what just happened.

What had just happened was the opening round in an all-out gang war. The theory that Baby Lane had shot Tupac later that night as payback for the assault almost immediately gained currency, due in large part to his obvious motivation. But the famed rapper was hardly the only victim in what would quickly escalate into a bloody free-for-all between Crips and Bloods in the months to come.

If anyone was in a position to track the blowback from the Tupac murder in the aftermath of the MGM Grand incident, it was Tim Brennan, who became actively involved in the case thanks to his expertise in Compton's gangs. Eager to assist the Las Vegas Police Department in their investigation, Brennan had written search warrants for several Compton gang safe houses, looking for any weapon that might have been used in Tupac's slaying. He drafted a lengthy Statement of Probable Cause, laying out in great detail the chain reaction of reprisal and retaliation that resulted from the events in Las Vegas.

According to Brennan's account, on September 9, two days after the murder, a Southside Crip kingpin named Darnell Brim was shot several times in the back on a Compton street. A stray bullet hit a ten-year-old girl, who was rushed to the hospital in critical condition, while later that evening persons unknown shot at another Crip, Orlando Lanier. Twelve hours later, Lanier's associate Bobby Finch was gunned down, even as Gary Williams, brother of Death Row Records security guard George Williams, was dispatched in a drive-by shooting.

Four days later two Mob Piru gangsters, Tyrone Lipscomb and David McMullen, were taken out in another drive-by, followed quickly by the shooting of Piru members Marcus Childs and Timothy Flanagan. Less than a week later the names of two more Crips, Gerode Mack and Johnny Burgie, were added to the bloody tally.

As the body count mounted, Bloods held a council of war in Leuders Park, a well-known gang hangout in Compton. On hand were representatives of a wide swathe of Compton Piru sets, including the Mob Piru, the Elm Lane Piru, the Fruit Town Piru, and the Cedar Block Piru. It was a rogues' gallery of gangsters with street names like "Lil Scar," "Tron," "Lil' Vent Dog," "Spook," "T-Spoon," and "O.G. Chism," who attended the conclave in a wheelchair. The message relayed by the Piru shot-callers to their troops was clear: anyone wearing Crips colors was fair game.

The Crips called their own war council, bringing together the Southside and Neighborhood Crips, along with the Kelly Park, Atlantic Drive, and Chester Street sets. In gangster parlance, it was on, and it would become one of the deadliest conflicts in Los Angeles gang history.

Given the distinct possibility that both Tupac and Biggie had been prime targets in the mayhem that had its origins in the Lakewood Mall and MGM Grand episodes, it made sense for Brennan and me to try to elicit more information from Tray. He had, after all, been a key player in both confrontations. The fact that more than a dozen years had passed since the events went down didn't improve our odds. If Tray had kept the truth to himself for so long, why would he talk to us now?

Our hope was that he might be willing to bargain information in exchange for leniency on the charge he was facing. I'd long since learned that when it comes to bad guys facing prison time, they all have a number in mind. That number is the length of a sentence beyond which they are willing to serve. For some, getting put away for two, four or even six years is no problem. Most gangsters have, after all, been in jail off and on their whole lives. To them, it's like a continuation of the old neighborhood, with friends and family members right there on the same cell block. But when the sentence begins to stretch into double digits they start to look for ways out, most commonly by assisting authorities in ongoing investigations. It's then that opportunities present themselves. But you also have to be careful. Facing stiff sentences, criminals have nothing to lose by telling you what they think you want to hear. Cutting deals with talkative convicts can be a treacherous business.

But it became apparent almost from the moment that Brennan and I showed up at the L.A. County Jail visiting room that we weren't going to get anywhere close to Tray's magic number. As soon as we started asking questions about the Lakewood Mall episode, we could almost see him shutting down in front of us. He didn't want to talk about it and wanted even less to talk about his connections to Suge Knight. At the mere mention of his name we could see, mixed with the stubbornness and suspicion in Tray's eyes, a flicker of fear. It was clear we were getting nowhere. We had come up empty on our first fishing expedition.

But it wasn't going to be our last. Given the dearth of any fresh information in the case we had no choice but to stick with our strategy of finding someone we could possibly turn. The next candidate to appear on our radar was named Corey Edwards, a Compton native with some solid connections to the Crip's upper echelons, including Baby Lane and his uncle, the drug dealer Keffe D.

Edwards had been present in Las Vegas the night of Tupac's death but his version of events had not proved especially enlightening. According to his statement, he had seen Baby Lane in a bar at the MGM Grand shortly after Tupac and his posse had beaten him up. "I walked over to him," Edwards recounts, "and asked him what had happened and if he was okay. He said that he had got into it with Tupac and Tupac's people, but that everything was cool. Baby Lane didn't appear to be injured or too upset about what happened."

It sounded like a standard evasion, especially considering that, in an earlier interview, he had remembered that Baby Lane, in the company of Keffe D, who also had been in Las Vegas for the prizefight, "was all mad and talking about getting back at the person who had jumped him." Edwards had obviously been tailoring his recollections to suit the evolving situation, but there were certain facts that were more difficult to finesse. "I don't consider myself a gang member," he told investigators with a straight face, "but I hang around all the neighborhood Southside Crips. Since we all grew up together, I consider them my friends."

It was, of course, a distinction without a difference. Whether or not Corey Edwards was a bone fide gangster, his criminal activity would have certainly qualified him for an honorary membership in any set. He had, for example, been singled out by the Drug Enforcement Agency, among others, for suspected cocaine trafficking. Edwards had, in fact, had a close call several years earlier in connection with the Tupac shooting. His associate, Bobby Finch, had become one of the first victims of the gang war sparked by the murder. Finch lived next door to Edwards in Compton and the word on the street was that the hit had really been intended for Corey. Despite his protests to the contrary, his close connection to the Crips had almost gotten him killed.

In August 2001, after an extensive investigation by federal authorities, Edwards was indicted in Columbus on cocaine conspiracy and money laundering charges. But before DEA agents could establish a link between Edwards and his suppliers, the suspect fled. He had been on the lam ever since. Given his close Southside associations, there was reason to believe that Corey Edwards might have inside information on the Biggie Smalls hit. Short of that, we could try to pry incriminating statements from him about associates who knew more than he did and bring them in to apply the same kind of pressure. Either way, he was worth talking to if we could find him, and that wasn't going to be easy. He had, for all intent and purpose, utterly vanished five years earlier, and there was no reason to think we'd have any better luck than the DEA agents who had been looking for him ever since.

But we did. Through real estate records we were able to locate the Corona, California, home of Lisa Garner, Corey Edwards's baby mama, who was caring for his elementary-school-age daughter. We staked out Garner's house and began some discreet questioning of neighbors, co-workers, and anyone who might have a connection to her and her fugitive boyfriend.

It was Daryn who struck pay dirt when a teacher of Edwards's little girl told him she would be celebrating her birthday at a local seafood franchise called Joe's Crab Shack. It seemed at least possible that Edwards would emerge from hiding long enough to make an appearance at the party. There was a hitch, however. At which of the many Crab Shacks in greater Los Angeles would the birthday take place? We checked a map and located the two closest to Garner's home. The night of the celebration we set up surveillance at both, but neither Edwards nor his family showed up at either one.

As the evening drew on, we racked out brains trying figure out where they might have gone instead. It was Daryn who came up with the idea of looking closer to Compton, Corey's old stomping ground. We found another Joe's Crab Shack outlet in Long Beach, not far away from his old neighborhood. Daryn and Alan Hunter hurried out to the location while I stayed behind at one of the other restaurants in case our quarry decided to show up.

Forty-five minutes later I got a call from Daryn. Edwards, along with much of his extended family, was on the premises. As the supervisor of the operation I told him to immediately move in and make an arrest. It was at that point that Hunter intervened. He had a better idea, he told me over the phone. They would wait for the party to break up and then trail Edwards out, meanwhile alerting the nearby Long Beach Sheriff's Department to pull him over once he was on the road.

I told Hunter what I thought of his plan in no uncertain terms. We had a fugitive drug dealer in our sights and the last thing I wanted to risk was a high-speed chase or worse should he attempt to escape. I felt bad that his daughter would have to see her father hauled away in handcuffs, but it couldn't be helped.

"You knew it would catch up with you sooner or later," remarked the birthday girl's grandfather as Daryn and a still-reluctant Hunter took Edwards into custody. He went quietly, offering no resistance, and, bright and early the next morning, Brennan and I went down to the City Jail at Parker Center to have a talk with him. We were hopeful that we'd get results this time. Edwards was in a world of trouble and it stood to reason that he'd be eager to cut a deal. Before long we deduced how he had managed to elude authorities for so long, mostly by using multiple fake driver's licenses, each of which was another possible count of up to three years in state prison for perjury. It was another bargaining chip we could use.

But it was all wishful thinking. Like Tray before him, Corey Edwards wasn't about to cooperate. He'd already given his statement, he told us. He was trying to go straight and start a new life as a boxing promoter. That was all he had to say on the subject. Like every criminal facing a prison sentence, he had done the math and was willing to take a calculated risk to find out what kind of time he would be facing back in Ohio. If the number came up right, he could wait it out. If it didn't, well, maybe he'd take us up on our offer to help him out if we could. We had hit another dry hole. We were now 0 for 2.

CHAPTER 10

Ballistics

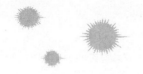

I T WASN'T VERY LONG AFTER the task force had been formed
that Tim Brennan was promoted to detective in the Sheriff's
Department and transferred out to another assignment. I was sorry to
see him go, but I could understand his desire to move on. Although
he was a good officer, methodical and thorough, it was clear early on
that he was not particularly well suited to the kind of broad based,
multi-agency investigation that we were mounting. A street cop,
accustomed to the exploits and action that came with the territory,
he was more comfortable chasing bad guys than plotting elaborate
strategies to crack a big and complex case. Gang life was what he
knew, and once he had relayed to us everything he could about the
subject, his usefulness was limited.

There was also the fact, because of his connection to the Compton
Police, that Brennan's efforts had been under a cloud long before
he was recruited to the team. The suspicion surrounding his loyalty

and motives were unfounded: Brennan was totally committed to catching bad guys. To that end, he had lent his expertise to the Las Vegas Metropolitan Police Department in their investigation of the Tupac shooting. Brennan had followed up his initial search warrant of Compton gang houses with another in May 1997, still looking for the gun used to kill the rapper. But by that time, it was clear that Las Vegas had gotten leery of Brennan and his persistent attempts to be part of the case.

The reason was simple and, at least indirectly, linked to the legacy of Russell Poole's investigation. Police from Compton had a tarnished reputation to say the least, all the more so since Poole had attempted to tie cops and Compton gangs together as part of a wider police conspiracy. Compton officers were stigmatized no matter how squeaky-clean they might be, and some of that suspicion was certainly justified. But Tim Brennan's professional integrity was the equal of any officer I'd ever known.

Not that it mattered. As the scope of gang involvement in the Tupac murder became increasingly apparent, the Las Vegas police adopted an ever more standoffish approach toward Brennan, concerned with the taint he might bring to their case. For his part, "Blondie" only wanted to give them the benefit of specialized knowledge and it must have been disheartening for him when it went unappreciated.

Before he left the task force, however, Brennan would prove to be extremely useful in another key area of our investigation. As part of our pursuit of individuals involved in the case on whom we could apply pressure, he'd been assigned the task of compiling files on every unsolved gang killing involving Mob Piru and Southside Crips that had occurred in L.A. County. Brennan detailed some twenty gang-related homicides. If we could arrest any of the perpetrators, we might just be able to leverage new information on the Biggie killing.

As Brennan's work progressed, he also uncovered nearly three hundred weapons, seized for a variety of reasons, but yet to be tested for ballistics evidence that might tie them to existing cases. The guns were stored in the evidence locker of the Sheriff's Department, transferred there after the Compton police force, thanks to the scandals that had engulfed it, was folded into county law enforcement operations.

It was in that weapons cache that Blondie came across a number of guns that caught our attention. They were .40s and 9mms, the same calibers used in the Tupac and Biggie shootings. It was here that the enhanced power that came with being a federal task force came in handy. We contacted the Bureau of Alcohol, Tobacco and Firearms, specifically Agent James Black, who agreed to test-fire the guns we were interested in. The ballistics procedure Black utilized involved discharging a round, recovering the shell casing, and making a digital image of the unique impression produced by the gun's firing pin. The image was then compared with millions of firing-pin patterns from shell casings recovered at various crime scenes and entered into the ATF's nationwide database.

Black almost immediately got a match with one of the .40s and when the news came in, the excitement in the task force headquarters was palpable: the test-fired casing matched that of a shell recovered in the Tupac murder case. It didn't escape our attention that the gun in question had been recovered in the yard of Lisa Garner's parents; the same Lisa Garner who was the girlfriend of the fugitive Corey Edwards. A family member had found the gun in Garner's backyard and had turned it in to the police. Edwards had admitted to being in Las Vegas the night of Tupac's murder. It all added up to what looked like our first major break in the case.

But there was a problem. In any criminal court case, the digital impression of a shell is not necessarily admissible evidence. What are needed to clinch a conviction based on ballistics evidence are the actual casings, from both the test firing and the crime scene. We had only one. The Las Vegas police had the other. Turf battles are regrettably common in law enforcement and we knew we couldn't just ask them to hand over the evidence we needed. Instead we sent them the gun in question, and asked them to test-fire it directly and compare the casings themselves.

The Las Vegas results came back negative: no match. It was baffling and more than a little frustrating. The chances of the two casing analyses coming up with contradictory results were slim. But our hands were tied. We couldn't very well ask LVMPD to test the gun again or, better yet, run an independent comparison. That would be tantamount to suggesting that they were either lying or incompetent and we had no reason to suspect that was the case. There was no way around it: protocol had to be observed. We were forced to let the promising lead languish, at least for the time being.

We had to look elsewhere and decided to make a third attempt to turn a potential witness for new information. The target this time was a full-on Crip named Michael "Owl" Dorrough, whose rap sheet included arrests for, among other charges, robbery, carrying a concealed weapon and murder. Once again, there was good reason to believe that he knew more than he had let on, especially as it pertained to Orlando "Baby Lane" Anderson.

Baby Lane himself was unavailable for interviews. In the months following the beating by Tupac and Suge's posse at the MGM Grand, the gangster had gained a reputation on the street as the mostly likely triggerman in the rapper's murder. He was seen as defending the honor of the Crips, but it turned out he was playing both sides. Anderson would subsequently give testimony in a parole violation hearing for Suge stemming from his participation in the assault at the MGM Grand. He insisted under oath that Knight had nothing to do with the attack, recalling that "He was the only one I heard saying, 'Stop this shit!'" Even the judge felt obliged to note for the record that the witness appeared to be lying through his teeth. It was shortly afterward that Baby Lane opened a well-appointed recording studio in Compton and began cutting tracks with local rappers under his start-up label, Success Records.

But Baby Lane's music-mogul dreams came to an abrupt end on May 25, 1998, when he and Dorrough, a close Crip associate, drove past a Compton strip mall. There, outside a car wash, they spotted a pair of Corner Pocket Crips, one of whom owed Baby Lane money. In an attempt to collect the debt, a gunfight erupted and all four men were hit in the hail of bullets. Fatally wounded, Baby Lane attempted to flee the scene, accompanied by the bleeding profusely Dorrough and leaving behind the dead Corner Pockets. After a few blocks the car rolled to a stop. An ambulance took the two to Martin Luther King Jr./Drew Medical Center, known as "Killer King" for the high rate of shooting victims that had expired there. Baby Lane was no exception. He was pronounced dead on the gurney.

Dorrough was subsequently tried and found guilty of all three homicides under the California felony murder rule, which stipulates that if a death occurs in the commission of a crime, the offender is automatically liable for murder, even if the death was incidental. Dorrough was convicted of triple homicide and given a triple-life sentence at Pelican Bay, the infamous maximum-security prison in Northern California.

In the minds of many, the violent end of Baby Lane was fitting payback for the murder of Tupac Shakur. But there was never anything more than circumstantial evidence linking him to the rapper's death. If he was indeed the shooter, the one person who might know was Michael Dorrough.

Along with Tim Brennan, on one of his last official tasks for the team, I went to Pelican Bay to interview Dorrough. It may seem a little strange, but I enjoy going to prisons. For one thing, there's a lot of history there, maybe not Pelican Bay, which was a relatively new, high-tech facility, but certainly in prisons like Folsom, which opened its gates way back in 1880 and houses California's original

Death Row. It's composed of two tiers of cells, four on top and four on the bottom. When a prisoner was scheduled for execution, he'd start out on the bottom right and move along from cell to cell as the ones ahead of him emptied out. Finally he'd be on the far left of the top tier, outside of which was a large overhead beam. When the time came, they'd take him out and hang him right there.

In contrast to the other thwarted interviews we had conducted, Dorrough was ready and willing to make a deal. He just wanted one thing in return. Knowing he had no chance of getting his triple murder sentence reduced, he was holding out instead for a transfer to Corcoran State Prison, where his father, likewise serving a life sentence, was housed. In exchange for the transfer, Dorrough promised to tell us about a purported meeting by Suge Knight, Baby Lane, and his uncle Keffe D Davis, that had supposedly occurred a few months after Tupac's murder.

In his convoluted version of events, Dorrough claimed that Puffy Combs had hired Baby Lane to kill Tupac Shakur, but that after the shooting Puffy had backed out of the deal and refused to pay the contract. A meeting was then called by Suge, during which it was proposed to pay Orlando what Puffy had promised if Baby Lane would take out Biggie. There was only one problem. The whole thing was a complete fabrication. It came unraveled when, monitoring the convict's phone calls, we heard him on the line instructing his cousin to go along with the story he was peddling to us. We'd struck out one more time. And we were running out of options.

CHAPTER 11

Keffe D

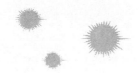

As 2006 WOUND DOWN and we began a new year of active investigation, the complex entanglements of the case became even more formidable. My original approach, to divide the investigation into separate probes on both the Crips and Bloods, helped to manage the amount of sheer information we were dealing with. But the fact was that we were running what amounted to two major cases at the same time, which required the task force to split it's focus. At the same time there were further personnel adjustments within the task force. We needed a Sheriff's Department replacement for the departing Tim Brennan and requested a homicide investigator to continue looking into the stack of unsolved killings he had compiled. They sent us Karen Shonka.

Relaxed and congenial, with a sharp eye for detail and a willingness to get her hands dirty, Karen was a welcome addition. But even with an able new member on the team, we were still feeling the pressure.

No one had set a deadline for us to solve the Biggie Smalls murder, but considering the amount of manpower and resources we had deployed, we knew it wasn't going to be an open-ended proposition. Sooner rather than later we would need to show results. Of course, police work doesn't unfold within predictable time frames. As our futile fishing expeditions had already established, a case could chase its own tail for weeks or months at a time before finally breaking. Someone once described war as long periods of boredom punctuated by intense bursts of action. That's a pretty apt description of detective work, too.

It wasn't until late 2007 that we saw our next burst of action. Part of the reason for the snail's pace of the investigation was simply that we didn't want to call unnecessary attention to our work. If word got out on the street that we were once again looking for the killer or killers of Biggie Smalls, and Tupac Shakur while we were at it, those who might be helpful would almost certainly get scared off. Our efforts had to appear routine, with no signs of urgency. We had to proceed with caution, cover our tracks, and, as much as possible, stay under the radar.

Yet, slowly but surely, we began to find our way forward, and by the early fall we had trained our sights on the one person who had been present at the scene of both the Biggie and Tupac murders, part of the Crips contingent in Las Vegas and a guest at the Petersen during the Vibe party. The name of Duane Keith "Keffe D" Davis was popping up over and over again as the scope of our investigation broadened.

The uncle of the deceased Baby Lane, Keffe D, along with his brother Kevin, was also one of the top shot-callers in the South Side Crips hierarchy, a hardheaded businessman who ran a high-volume narcotics manufacturing and distribution operation. Over the course of two decades he had racked up an impressive rap sheet, including numerous felony arrests for possession with intent to sell, and in 1997 he had become the target of a major federal narcotics investigation.

The case exposed an extensive network headed by Keefe D, with Kevin Davis as second in command, overseeing a squad of Compton-based dealers who went by such names as "Doonie" and "P-Rain," "Fly" and "Big Dog." The crew handled transactions measured in multiple kilos, and tens of thousands of dollars changed hands on a weekly basis. Federal wiretaps recorded the constant use of the term "glazed donuts" to signify an ounce of cocaine, and the investigation further revealed that Davis and his gang were expert "flippers," kiting money provided by one buyer to finance other deals. Convicted on multiple narcotics counts, Davis received a four-year sentence.

After serving his time, Davis immediately went back to business, with expansion plans that dwarfed his previous operation. Short and stocky, with a salt-and-pepper goatee and his trademark gapped front teeth, Keffe D, in partnership with his brother, would do much in the years that followed to take the Crips criminal enterprise nationwide, with a wide-ranging network of franchised drug dealers. Naturally, Keffe D had been in our sights from the inception of the task force. If we could figure out a way to flip him there could be a huge potential pay-off, but as with every element in the case, we needed to tread lightly to allay any suspicions that we were targeting him.

Unfortunately, not everyone in the task force was on the same page. Early on in the investigation Alan Hunter, and another detective on loan to us from the LAPD had taken it upon themselves to try and single-handedly deliver Keffe D. Without advising Tyndall or any of the other supervisory staff, they sought out Kevin Davis in hopes of pressuring him for information on his brother. When he proved uncooperative, Hunter and his partner left a police business card and departed. A few hours later Tyndall received a phone call from Keffe D's attorney Edi Faal, who had previously defended alleged gang members, including Orlando Anderson. I had had a run-in with Faal during an alleged false-arrest case that had been summarily tossed out of court. That encounter had left me leery of the high profile lawyer.

Faal's message to Tyndall was clear: his client, Duane Keith Davis, didn't want to talk to the police for any reason, at any place and at any time. If we have anything to say to him, we say it to Faal. Before we clocked out that day, the LAPD detective, who'd been the ranking officer on the botched attempt, had been asked to leave the task force.

Keffe D now knew we were looking for him, which meant he would be all that much harder to find, and more frustrating months would pass before we discovered another way to make a move on him. Because of our federal status we had access to the extensive Drug Enforcement Agency database, from which we learned of an ongoing investigation out of Richmond, Virginia, that directly involved both Keith and Kevin Davis.

The DEA had been tracking a drug-running business that the brothers had set up between Compton and Richmond, involving a large contingent of middlemen, including the Southside Crip Leon "Dirt Rock" Hammond, who had been present at the Lakewood Mall during the now-infamous theft of the Death Row medallion. Another key figure in the Richmond case was Pedro Hill, who had become an unusually talkative defendant after his arrest in early 2007. Hill would provide the DEA with a richly detailed account of the drug ring's operations, naming "Cali Kev," aka Kevin Davis, as his Los Angeles cocaine connection. Kevin, Hill told the DEA, ran a vintage-car restoration business as an elaborate front for moving merchandise by shipping vehicles back east stuffed with cocaine in their tires. Unrestored cars would make the return trip packed with money.

Hill arranged with Cali Kev to make several such shipments to Richmond in early 2006, the last for two hundred kilos, discounted to $19,000 apiece in consideration of Hill's status as a valued customer. Pedro was, in fact, treated to a dazzling stay in Hollywood on his next trip to the coast, put up in a swank hotel and taken backstage for a concert at the House of Blues to see the Death Row rapper Snoop Dogg. He also had an opportunity to meet Keffe D and would go on to tell authorities that the brothers didn't see eye to eye when it came to running the business. Kevin, Hill claimed, was doing all the work, while Keffe D was resting on his laurels as a respected "Original Gangster," who had used his influence and connections to set up the network.

Once we caught wind of the DEA's developing case out of Richmond we got in touch with the investigators to coordinate our efforts. We were particularly interested in their developing case against Dirt Rock, who, as a courier for the ring, would shortly be facing federal charges of drug trafficking and money laundering. Given that Keffe D, by virtue of his "O.G." status, was one step removed from the daily operation of the ring, it was going to be difficult for the DEA to pin charges on him. We needed to engineer an operation to reel him in and compel his cooperation. Dirt Rock was facing some significant prison time, and it was clear from our first meeting with him in early September 2007 that the possible sentence would far exceed the magic number we needed to get him working on our side. Our approach was simple and direct: we wanted Dirt Rock to buy drugs from Keffe D, the more the better. But we also knew that, as a lowly mule, he would immediately raise suspicions if he approached Keffe D waving a wad of cash for a big buy. Instead, we decided, he would pose as a go-between. All we needed was a credible customer.

We had a perfect candidate in mind. He was a CS (confidential source) that the ATF's Jim Black and I had frequently used in the past, specifically to make drug purchases from suspected dealers. He would pose as our buyer while Dirt Rock assumed the role of broker.

It wasn't until early 2008 that we had all the pieces in place and put Dirt Rock on a wiretapped call to set up a meeting with Keffe D, telling him that he had a potential buyer for "one of those Kentucky Fried Chickens." It was yet another code phrase, this time signifying a kilo of coke. Keffe D was amenable to the arrangement, going so far as to suggest that Dirt Rock's customer might also be interested in purchasing some "Arrowhead Water," a reference to the potent and volatile street drug phencyclidine, more commonly known as PCP and sold in liquid form. There was only one condition: Keffe D wanted to meet the buyer. Accordingly, Dirt Rock and the CS arrived for a formal introduction at an apartment in a neighborhood bordering Compton.

"Are you bringing the contract with you?" Davis had asked over his tapped line when Hammond called ahead to announce their arrival. The "contract" was $16,800 in DEA funds parceled out in thousand-dollar bundles carried by the CS in a bag. Assured they had the money, Keffe D produced a tightly wrapped parcel of high-grade "Kentucky Fried Chicken." The deal was done with a promise of others, including the PCP Davis had mentioned, to come.

We were on our way, but it was imperative not to act precipitously and push for another drug deal too soon. As spring turned to summer, we bided our time, keeping tabs on Keffe D through constant surveillance and a wiretap, allowing us to chronicle his numerous drug deals and at the same time compile a complete list of his customers. For good measure, we hid a GPS transmitter on the undercarriage of his Lexus to track his movements. We were trying, as much as possible, to build an airtight case that would meet federal guidelines for a life sentence. The simple truth was that we needed to leverage Keffe D's cooperation. The only way to do that, to compel him to tell the truth, was to present him with a credible threat of life in prison. The reality is that a majority of crimes are solved and criminals apprehended by just such methods, by using bad guys against each other, creating a situation in which we can catch them doing what they do. We never forced Keffe D to sell drugs. We simply facilitated a routine transaction that we could then use as evidence against him. That's how you catch criminals.

But in order for our plan to work, we had to build an airtight case that would meet federal guidelines for a life sentence and clinch our bargaining power when the time came. In order to accomplish that, we had to meet a threshold of quantity the feds had established for any major drug prosecution. Eventually we were able to fulfill that requirement when Dirt Rock arranged with Keffe D for the sale of a gallon of PCP. The drug is so dangerous and deadly that its users commonly called it "Embalming Fluid," and a large amount would automatically meet federal guidelines. A gallon of PCP is potentially

Duane "Keffe D" Davis (in hat) and his nephew Orlando Anderson (far right) with their Southside Crips crew. Davis and Anderson would later participate in the killing of Tupac Shakur.

worth hundreds of thousands of dollars when sold on the streets in individually soaked cigarettes called "Shermans" after the preferred brand of smokes.

Dirt Rock had once again arranged the deal with our Confidential Source acting as the buyer. In the garage of a Compton bungalow, Keffe D handed over a gallon jug inside a plastic bag. Dirt Rock opened it and, smelling the amber-colored contents, recoiled. There was no mistaking the noxious odor of Embalming Fluid. For $10,500, provided once again by the DEA, the deal was done.

CHAPTER 12

The Sit Down

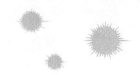

With the various drug deals we had set in motion, combined with his prior convictions, we were confident that we could dangle a twenty-five-years-to-life sentence over Keffe D; great incentive for him to spill whatever he knew about whatever we wanted to know. Everything was in place for what we hoped would be a major breakthrough in the case.

Meanwhile, we moved in to clear up the PCP operation that our wiretaps and surveillance had exposed. We had been able to identify Keffe D's supplier, a major manufacturer under investigation by the Texas DEA, which reached out to us when it discovered that our cases were converging. With their assistance we raided his PCP and meth lab and promptly extradited the suspect back to Texas to face charges.

Accompanying us on the raid was Detective Frank Lyga of the LAPD, who shot Kevin Gaines in the infamous 1997 road rage incident that had prompted Russell Poole's initial conjectures of a police conspiracy. Beyond that unwelcome notoriety, Lyga also happened to be one of the nation's foremost experts on illegal drug labs. It was his compelling testimony that helped to convict the drug manufacturer.

Moving in on our primary target, Daryn Dupree and I manned a stakeout at the Corona home of Paula Davis, Keffe D's wife, monitoring activity from a car parked down the street. It wasn't long before our wait was rewarded when Keffe D ambled out, carrying trash bags to the curb. We watched him go back inside, and a moment later the automatic garage door swung open and his black Lexus pulled out into the driveway. We moved quickly, blocking the car's exit and approaching it on both sides. But Keffe D wasn't behind the wheel. Instead we found his wife, Paula, glaring at us through the tinted glass.

"Where's your husband?" I asked when she rolled down the window.

"He's not here," she answered defiantly.

"That's funny," Daryn interjected, "because we just saw him take out the trash."

"I tell you what," I continued, in my soothing and reasonable "good cop" voice. "Why don't you go back inside and tell him we're here. Let him know we're not going to arrest him. We just want to talk."

Paula got out of the car and hurried back into the house through the access door at the rear of the garage. Daryn and I waited for a few minutes in the driveway, alert to any possibility. Keffe D was an authentic gangster, a powerful man accustomed to enforcing his will. We were invading his inner sanctum, tucked away in a pleasant middle-class housing development, far from the mean streets of Compton. Under the circumstances, anything could happen.

Finally, the door through which Paula had disappeared opened again and Keffe D emerged. I have to admit that seeing him in the flesh made an impression on me. For so long he had only been a name in a file; a character in stories spun by sources; a voice at the other end of a wiretapped line. Now, suddenly, we were face to face and I could see in his heavyset features a full range of emotions: fear, anger, and even a kind of resignation, as if he'd been expecting this moment for a long time.

"Do we have to do this on the street?" he asked plaintively, looking up and down the block to see if the neighbors were peeking out from behind their kitchen curtains.

Daryn suggested we move into the garage and we crossed into the cool, dimly lit interior. Keffe D punched the button behind us to shut the heavy door. He took three folding chairs from a corner and, opening them, set them out in the middle of the concrete floor. We sat down and, just at that moment, the lights went out, plunging the garage into pitch darkness.

My hand instinctively went for my gun. Had we been set up? Had he trapped us in the garage? I could hear a sharp intake of breath from Daryn, sitting next to me, and then a scraping sound as Keffe D got to his feet. What seemed like an endless stretch of silence followed until the lights suddenly flickered back on and we saw him standing at the automatic shutoff switch, turning the timer back on. I glanced over at Daryn. His hand was inside his jacket, resting on his service weapon, just like mine was. We started to breathe again.

Keffe D moved back to take his seat and in the next few minutes we laid it out for him: the surveillance, the wiretaps, the drug deals, the federal narcotics rap and the stiff sentence that would come with it. In the interests of protecting our informants, we deliberately steered clear of the specific details of the evidence we had gathered. But it was a fine line between telling him too much and not telling him enough and, in the end, he didn't seem entirely convinced we had an airtight case against him. We could see that from the skeptical glint in his eye.

"You think it over," Daryn said as we both stood up, preparing to leave. "And get yourself a lawyer."

"But let me give you a word of advice," I added, handing him my business card. "If you're thinking of being represented by Edi Faal, think again. You need to know up front that we're not going to work with him. Find someone else."

Keffe D rose and hit the button to open the garage door. Sunshine flooded in and we squinted against the bright light. His skepticism had begun to fade. He was thinking now, figuring the angles and weighing his options. "What do you want from me?" he asked at last.

I paused on my way to the car and turned to him. "Let me put it this way," I replied. "We're homicide investigators."

It was less than an hour later, while we were still driving back to the task force headquarters, that my cell phone rang. On the line was an attorney named Wayne Higgins, whose reputation for integrity put him in a different league from Edi Faal. Higgins was one of those rare lawyers whose concern for his client was tempered by his interest in justice being served. Keffe D had a new lawyer, one who was open to negotiation. It was a good sign.

In response to Higgins's request, we filled him in on the outlines of the case, at the same time suggesting that the best course of action might be a meeting between the parties concerned at everyone's earliest convenience. By two o'clock that afternoon, Higgins, Keffe D, Daryn, and I were sitting around a large table in the conference room of Assistant U.S. Attorney Timothy Searight's office.

We let Searight take the lead. In a reasoned, modulated tone he explained in detail the scope of the case we had against Keith Davis and the probable life sentence that came with it. Keffe D and Higgins listened impassively, and then requested some time alone to discuss their options. We left the room and fifteen minutes later were summoned back. Higgins announced that his client was ready to cooperate with us.

It was, all in all, a banner day for the investigation. After so many false starts and dead ends, we had finally achieved our goal of putting a potentially key witness under pressure to tell us something we didn't already know. And it wasn't just any witness. It was Keffe D. He'd been on hand for the deaths of both Tupac Shakur and Biggie Smalls and was uniquely positioned to dispel the decade's worth of rumor and innuendo that had grown up like weeds around the murders. We were, understandably, optimistic.

Searight ended the meeting with the possibility of putting forward a formal proffer, a government assurance of consideration in Keffe D's case in exchange for his cooperation. What didn't need spelling out were the stringent terms of a formal proffer. Keffe D and his attorney both knew it had to be the whole truth and nothing but. Anything Keffe D would tell us would need to be corroborated by another, independent source. If, in the process of confirming his story, we discovered that he was lying to us about even the smallest detail, all bets were off and the proffer would be null and void.

It was coming up on Thanksgiving, 2008, more than two long years since the task force had been formed. We were on the verge of a major break in the case and wanted to savor the moment. We also wanted to give Keffe D chance to think long and hard about doing the right thing. For those reasons, I suggested a time out. "Go home," I told Keffe D that afternoon in Searight's office. "Enjoy the holiday with your family. Then we can get down to business." It was also decided that, in deference to Higgins, all future interviews would take place at the attorney's Beverly Hills offices. On that magnanimous note the meeting broke up and we arranged to reconvene in mid-December.

In the interim, news of our progress spread like wildfire through law enforcement ranks. Considering Keffe D's stature in the South Side Crips—one of our informants consistently referred to him as the "president" of the gang—it seemed as if everyone, from Robbery-Homicide to Narcotics to the Sheriff's Department, had one or more unsolved cases that they were certain Keffe D could help clear up. It was evident from the onset that our witness would be doing a lot of talking. But it was crucial from the standpoint of simple manageability that the interviews would need to be tightly controlled. I immediately made it clear that, once we had gotten what we needed from our star informant, other interviews would be doled out on a strict need-to-know basis, methodically covering one subject at a time.

It was in this period that I pretty much took over investigative control of the task force. I had been front and center, along with Daryn, in the effort to reel in Keffe D. The work was made easier by the fact that Tyndall had recently retired and Holcomb was soon to follow. Accordingly, I was promoted to head the task force. Of course, there was still a chain of command to which I was responsible, not to mention the political considerations of the case that needed constant tending. But with Keffe D now cooperating I was pretty much calling the shots. Daryn Dupree was, in all practical respects, my partner on the case and officers Trujillo and Bazulto were proving their worth on a daily basis. Alan Hunter, meanwhile, seemed to be intent on alienating himself from the team, declining repeated offers to participate. From here on out, I needed to keep close tabs on the internal dynamics of the team, which was now, to all intent and purposes, under my supervision.

Shortly before our follow-up meeting with Keffe D, I received a call from Higgins. He had a simple question: what exactly was the nature of the information we were seeking from his client? I was equally direct in my response: we'd want to know what really happened outside the Petersen Museum on the night of March 9, 1997. In short, who killed Biggie Smalls and why?

It was a question that hung in the air as Bill Holcomb, Daryn Dupree, the FBI's Special Agent Jeff Bennett, and I made our way through the plush lobby of the Beverly Hills high-rise where Wayne Higgins did business. It was 10:30 on a clear, crisp morning, the sun just beginning to break through a wintery haze as we emerged from the elevator, which emptied into a hallway leading to the lawyer's office.

Looming in the corridor, outside the conference room where our sit-down would take place, was Keffe D himself, dressed casually in a t-shirt and jeans. I stood next to him, nodding a slight greeting as we waited to be escorted in.

After a moment he leaned over to me and, in a low voice, spoke close to my ear. "I don't know nothin' about what you want to talk to me for," he said. "But what I do know is gonna blow your fuckin' mind."

PART
FOUR

CHAPTER 13

Who Shot Ya?

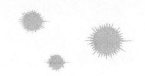

Tupac Shakur would never be riding higher than on the evening of September 7, 1996, cruising through a blazing galaxy of lights along the Las Vegas Strip in a brand new black BMW 750 sedan driven by Suge Knight.

The sunroof of the Beemer was open to the sky and hip-hop pounded from the car's state-of-the-art speakers, echoing across the vast desert. A phalanx of support and security vehicles formed a convoy down Las Vegas Boulevard in heavy Saturday-night traffic and the wide street quickly became an impromptu parade route as passing pedestrians immediately recognized the superstar rapper. Photoflashes flared and gang signs were thrown up in triumphant salute to the man whose music had become the soundtrack to an era.

All Eyez on Me, Tupac's Grammy-nominated third album, had been released seven months earlier and by April of that year had already sold five million albums, on its way to an astonishing total of nearly ten million. By a wide margin one of the most successful rap recordings in history, *All Eyez On Me* was also among a handful of the best-selling albums of the decade, in line with iconic releases by Michael Jackson, Eric Clapton, Pearl Jam, and, tellingly, the Notorious B.I.G. The singles "How Do U Want It" and "All About U" had been everywhere that summer, proclaiming not just the ascendancy of a major new star, but also the mainstreaming of a sound straight from the street that had lost none of its potent authenticity in the transition. Tupac Shakur was the real deal, a natural-born performer whose enormous charisma and innate intelligence put him in line to become a spokesman for a whole generation of young blacks looking for a leader.

Catapulting off the success of *All Eyez on Me*, Tupac had recently completed his follow-up Death Row release, written, recorded, and mixed in less than two weeks during August 1996. *The Don Killuminati: The 7 Day Theory* contained a cut titled "Bomb First," which featured the sounds of seven shots being fired. As the last report faded in the mix, Tupac emerged as his swaggering new alter ego, Makaveli. As creative strategy, Tupac's lightning-fast recording pace and shape-shifting identity suggested a supremely confident artist at the top of his game. But *Don Killuminati* was a darker and far less accessible work than its predecessor. On track after track he called out his rivals in rap, disrespecting by name everyone from Biggie Smalls and Puff Daddy to his former producer, Dr. Dre. It was as if Tupac could not tolerate another star burning brighter than his own.

And that night on Las Vegas Boulevard, none did. Conclusive proof of his exalted status was breaking out in spontaneous displays by an adoring public as Suge drove on a roundabout route toward their destination: a purple-hued nightspot at 1700 East Flamingo Road. Owned by Suge, it was dubbed Club 662, for the numbers on a phone pad that spell out MOB. It was here that Tupac was scheduled to perform, at a charity event benefiting a local gym founded by a former Las Vegas police officer to steer kids away from violence. But there was more to Tupac's appearance on stage than simple altruism: it was part of a community-service deal Suge's lawyers had negotiated to mitigate some of Tupac's myriad legal entanglements.

The event promised a standing room only crowd, with word getting around that night that the newly crowned heavyweight champion, Mike Tyson, barely winded by his 109-second bout with Bruce Seldon, would be dropping by. There was a special relationship between the fighter and the rapper, in evidence earlier that evening at the main event in the MGM Grand arena, when the PA pumped out the driving hip-hop track "Write the Glory," which Tupac had penned especially for Tyson. Tupac beamed from his thousand dollar ringside seat as his amplified rap blasted through the darkened hall. It didn't get any better than that.

And it had been worse, a lot worse. A little less than two years earlier, on November 30, 1994, Shakur had been shot multiple times, severely beaten, robbed, and left for dead in the lobby of a New York City recording studio. It was an incident many would claim had lit the spark on the murderous bicoastal rap wars that were still raging the night Tupac and Suge made their exultant way toward Club 662.

At the time of the assault, Tupac had already riveted the rap world with his 1991 debut album, *2Pacalypse Now*. A rising star in every sense of the term, Tupac was much in demand as a guest vocalist on recordings by other artists. That night he was scheduled to perform on a track by the young hip-hop hopeful Little Shawn for the hefty sum of $7,000.

The deal had been initiated by Little Shawn's manager, James "Jimmy Henchman" Rosemond, a formidable New York gang member who had transformed himself into a respectable businessman, starting Czar Entertainment and, in the process, earning a reputation as what Vibe called "one of the most feared players in hip-hop." Over the course of several months Rosemond had worked hard to ingratiate himself with Tupac in hopes of eventually adding the rapper to his client roster. Part of his strategy was to encourage Tupac to leave his label, Interscope Records, and sign instead with Puffy Combs's Bad Boy imprint. But Tupac had repeatedly rebuffed his overtures with a kind of offhanded disdain that rubbed Rosemond the wrong way.

Rosemond had earlier introduced Shakur to another shadowy East Coast underworld figure, Jacques "Haitian Jack" Agnant, and the pair had hit it off, running a wild streak through New York City in late 1993. A little too wild, according to the testimony of a nineteen year-old fan who accused Tupac and Haitian Jack, along with two other men, of gang-raping her in a luxury suite at the Parker Meridien Hotel. Arrested for the assault, Tupac had returned to New York to stand trial on the charges a year later.

By then, Jimmy Henchman and Puffy Combs had supposedly laid plans to cut Tupac down to size. His refusal to sign with Combs's company was seen by many as a direct insult to the music mogul and Tupac's frequent and very public affronts to Puffy and his organization had only fueled the fire. A trap had been laid with the $7,000 recording fee as bait. Or so the story went.

Shakur arrived for the gig at Quad Recording Studios on Seventh Avenue, where Rosemond had booked time for the Little Shawn sessions. Whether by accident or design a large group of Bad Boy executives, including Puffy Combs, had gathered in the adjacent studio for a playback of tracks on the debut album by Biggie Smalls' pet project, Junior M.A.F.I.A..

Entering the lobby in the company of his manager, Fred Moore, and a friend, Randy "Stretch" Walker, Tupac and his associates were approached by three men dressed in army fatigues, who demanded that Tupac and the others hand over their expensive jewelry. When Tupac refused, a pistol whipping ensued, at which point the rapper pulled out his own gun, accidently shooting himself in the groin in the process. A flurry of gunfire erupted and Tupac was hit four more times, taking bullets in his head, hand, and leg. Bleeding profusely, he dropped to the floor, where he was kicked, punched, and relieved of a medallion valued at $40,000. The assailants vanished into the night, pursued by a wounded Fred Moore until he, too, collapsed. Meanwhile, Tupac rode the elevator to the tenth floor studio, where the door opened on Puffy and his Bad Boy cadre. Their shocked expressions at the sight of Tupac, bloody but still standing, were ultimately accorded a variety of interpretations.

Paramedics rushed Tupac to Bellevue Hospital, where he was operated on for three hours. His condition somewhat stabilized, he was admitted to intensive care. There, in the early morning hours of November 30, he checked himself out, apparently still in fear for his life. A few days later, bandaged and in a wheelchair with a frightened look in his eyes, Tupac arrived at court to hear the verdict on the Parker Meridien rape case. The jury swiftly convicted him of first-degree sexual abuse. He was sentenced to a four-and-a-half-year prison term.

Considering the ultimate outcome of the Quad attack, it's hardly surprising that it has been seen as the flash point in ensuing gang wars. It was a conflict that at first had been carried out only in mocking taunts, nasty but hardly lethal. In the late spring of 1995, the Notorious B.I.G. released "Who Shot Ya?" and although both the artist and Puffy Combs, the track's producer, would insist that the song had been recorded months before the slaughter on Seventh Avenue, there are more than enough provocative lyrics in the track to suggest otherwise. Aside from such vivid descriptive verses as *"It's on, nigga / fuck all that bickering beef / I can hear sweat trickling down your cheek,"* the song's fade seemed, to many, as a de facto admission of responsibility. *"You rewind this,"* Biggie rumbled, *"Bad Boy's behind this."* Tupac would eventually respond in kind on "Hit 'Em Up," rife with such incendiary rhymes as *"Who shot me / But your punks didn't finish / Now you 'bout to feel the wrath of a menace."* But by that time, the war had escalated far beyond words.

The escalation had begun in the summer of 1995 when Death Row Records founder Suge Knight began regular visits to Tupac at the Dannemora maximum security prison in upstate New York. He would eventually post $1.4 million in bail, freeing the rapper and funding his appeal on the rape conviction. Tupac reciprocated by signing an exclusive recording contract with Death Row, demonstrating in no uncertain terms to which coast, and to what gang, he now pledged allegiance. Tupac had undergone a startling transformation behind bars. The inspirational aspect of his artistry had been replaced by dark and violent imagery, tinged with paranoia and bent on revenge. It was a side of the twenty-four-year-old rapper that many felt had been brought out by his association with Suge Knight.

For his part, the rapper, like his new mentor, made no secret of whom he held responsible for his near-death experience in the Quad Studios lobby. The track "Against All Odds," on *Don Killuminati*, would implicate Puffy by name and promise payback to, among others, Jimmy Henchman. At that time, however, Rosemond was safe from retribution, behind bars on a laundry list of drug and weapons charges.

Others were not so lucky. In September of that year Suge's friend and enforcer, Jake Robles was shot and killed at the Platinum Club in Atlanta, Georgia, a hit that, according to a 1997 issue of *Spin Magazine*, Knight pinned on one of Puffy's bodyguards. It was a charge Combs would vehemently counter in the pages of *Vibe*. "I went to Atlanta with my son," he asserted, "…I didn't even have bodyguards, so that's a lie that I did."

Three months later and a year to the day after the Quad ambush, Tupac's associate "Stretch" Walker, was shot dead on a Queens street. It is a homicide that, like so many other incidents surrounding the recording studio ambush, has never been solved. But its ripple effects would continue to be felt for years afterward, down to 2008, at the same time as our task force was deep into the resurrected investigation of the Biggie Smalls homicide and, by extension, the death of Tupac Shakur. It was in March of that year that the *Los Angeles Times* published a bombshell article purporting to have uncovered new and incriminating information about the Quad Studios attack fourteen years earlier. Chuck Philips, a highly respected Pulitzer Prize-winning journalist who covered the music industry, filed the story. His account leaned heavily on a description of events laid out in an FBI report from a confidential source, claiming that Puffy Combs had indeed been behind the assault on Tupac. The unnamed source also went on to implicate Jimmy Henchman, Haitian Jack, and a wannabe gangster named James Sabatino. The FBI document detailing these revelations was duly posted on the newspaper's website.

There was only one problem. As the *Smoking Gun* website quickly discovered, the report was a complete fabrication. It was James Sabatino, using a prison typewriter and photocopier, who had assembled it for the sole purpose of putting himself in the middle of the action.

Sabatino had long boasted of being a member of Bad Boy's inner circle, supposedly planning lavish parties for Combs, using fake credit cards to charge hotels, choppers, and limos. He was eventually convicted of wire fraud and racketeering and sent to jail, where he concocted the fake FBI reports that Philips had used as the basis of his explosive story. Sabatino was something of a pathological liar, at least according to his father, who characterized him as a "disturbed young man who needed attention like a drug." Philips, who had devoted years of intensive investigative journalism to the Biggie and Tupac murders, had been taken in by a forgery, and an inept forgery at that. *The Smoking Gun* pointed out in its analysis of the purported FBI document that, among other inconsistencies, the Bureau had not used typewriters for thirty years and there were also typos and misspellings "remarkably similar" to those found in the court documents Sabatino had previously filed. "The *Times* appears to have been hoaxed by an imprisoned con man," *The Smoking Gun* concluded, "an audacious swindler who created a fantasy world in which he managed hip-hop luminaries."

"In relying on documents that I now believe were fake," Chuck Philips subsequently admitted in a statement, "I failed to do my job." There was no such dereliction of duty on the part of attorneys for Puffy and Jimmy Henchman. Combs's lawyer claimed that the newspaper's conduct met the legal standard for "actual malice," while Rosemond's attorney was even more to the point. "I would suggest that Mr. Philips and his editors...take out their checkbooks."

Like Russell Poole before him, Chuck Philips had been taken down by a case that now richly deserved its reputation for being cursed. Biggie Smalls and Tupac Shakur were dead and gone. But they were a very long way from being forgotten.

CHAPTER 14

662

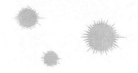

AS TUPAC AND SUGE CRUISED down the Vegas Strip on their way to some hard partying, the nightmare of the last few years must have seemed like a distant memory. The mogul had delivered on all the promises he had made while Tupac was in jail. Tupac was now selling records and concert tickets in staggering numbers and had a firm foothold in Hollywood thanks to his roles in the twin hits *Poetic Justice* (1992) and *Above the Rim* (1994). He was a bigger star with a brighter future by a mind-boggling order of magnitude.

The ongoing gang war he had helped to incite only served to fuel his outsized ego. Only a few hours earlier he and his Piru posse had dealt a painful lesson to Baby Lane in the lobby of the MGM Grand, punishing the Crip for the crime of stealing a Death Row medallion at the Lakewood Mall two months earlier. For Tupac, art now imitated life: the "Thug Life" that he celebrated in song and played to the hilt as a world-class celebrity outlaw. He was at the absolute pinnacle of his life and career. There was no place left to go and nothing standing in his way of getting there.

After the Tyson-Seldon bout, Tupac had returned to the suite at the Luxor Hotel he shared with Kidada Jones, daughter of the music impresario Quincy Jones and sister of QD3, the producer of several tracks on *The Don Killumanti*. An off-and-on girlfriend at the time, Kidada was serving as Tupac's consort for the Vegas weekend, and she listened as Tupac bragged about the thrashing he had just given Baby Lane, even as he took his time selecting a change of clothes. He had decided to go casual, picking out a black-and-white tank top, baggy blue jeans, and the regulation gold Death Row necklace for his night on the town. Kidada, instinctively wary of potential blowback from the beating, declined to accompany him.

Conspicuously absent in Tupac's attire was the bulletproof Kevlar vest he wore as protection against the many enemies—real and imagined—he had accumulated on his rise to the top. He didn't need it, he had earlier told Kidada as they had packed for the trip. After all, Vegas was hot and dry and the flak jacket would be uncomfortable and, more to the point, noticeably bulky. Sin City was, he believed, far removed from the gang violence of the East and West Coasts and the last thing Tupac wanted was to create the impression that he had something to fear.

Leaving Kidada to make her own plans for the evening, Tupac descended to the Luxor's sweeping driveway, where the evening's convoy had already arrived. His entourage was the standard assortment of flacks, flunkies, and hangers-on, as well as a hefty security presence, including Tupac's bodyguard for the event, Frank Alexander, one-time bodybuilder and former reserve deputy for the Orange County Sheriff's Department. Also on duty was the ex-Compton police officer Reginald Wright, Jr., head of Wright Way Protective Services, a security firm financed by Suge Knight specifically to provide muscle for Death Row. Since the necessary out-of-state permits had not been obtained, none of the Wright Way guards present that night were armed.

The half dozen vehicles, with Suge and Tupac in the lead, made their way over to the prestigious Paradise Valley township on the city's outskirts, where Suge Knight kept a home. There, Knight also changed for the evening, and at about ten o'clock the group headed out again, heading for Club 662. It took them the better part of an hour to reach the south end of the Strip, through bumper-to-bumper traffic and the fast-gathering crowd along the sidewalks, clamoring for pictures and autographs. Just after eleven, Suge was pulled over by a LVMPD officer on a bicycle. The brand-new car displayed no temporary plates, the cop told him, also informing him that the volume on the car stereo was too loud. After a brief exchange, Suge was let go without being ticketed.

Shortly afterward a rented convertible Sebring pulled up along-side Suge and Tupac. Inside the Chrysler were four female friends out from Los Angeles for a weekend of fun. Among them was Ingrid Johnson, who recognized Suge from a brief encounter some four years earlier. She caught Knight's attention and he invited the group along to Club 662 as his guests. The procession continued, the Sebring keeping pace with the BMW as it turned off Las Vegas Boulevard east onto Flamingo Road. A mile farther on they stopped for a red light at Koval Lane. The BMW carrying Tupac and Suge was in the center lane, one lane over from Johnson and her companions. Other vehicles in the convoy had pulled up directly behind the idling BMW, effectively boxing in the lead car.

It was then, as they waited for the light to change, that Ingrid Johnson heard gunshots, a lot of gunshots. "Drive on!" she shouted to her friend behind the wheel. "Drive on!" The convertible squealed across the intersection, making a sharp right and narrowly avoiding another vehicle making the same turn. When questioned later, she would be able to identify it only by its color: white.

It was a late-model Cadillac. Unnoticed, it had eased down Flamingo Road past the security contingent and pulled along the right side of the BMW. According to other eyewitnesses, four black men were paired off in the front and back seats. It was the rider in the right rear seat of the Caddy, leaning over the passenger next to him, who had opened up with a semiautomatic handgun, spraying the right side of the 750, riddling the door and shattering the heavily tinted windows.

"All I saw was the position of the shooter," the bodyguard Frank Alexander would later recount, describing his perspective from the car immediately behind the Beemer. "He was in the backseat. I saw the arm of the shooter come out. I saw a silhouette of him, which was a black person wearing a skull cap, a beanie cap."

Directly in the withering line of fire, Tupac tried desperately to scramble out of the way, but was held in place, a stationary target, by his seat belt. As he twisted around trying to escape the spray of bullets, he exposed his torso and was immediately struck in the chest, as well as his right hip, arm, and hand: four hits at close range, all in quick succession. "Get down!" Suge bellowed, grabbing the rapper and trying to pull him back into his seat before being clipped himself in the head and neck with shrapnel and glass fragments.

Meanwhile, Alexander had leaped from his car and was running toward the BMW, spattered now by thirteen slugs. As he approached, the car suddenly lurched to the left. In a desperate maneuver Suge had yanked the wheel into a sharp U-turn, riding on two blown-out tires as he sped back down Flamingo Road. Alexander hurried back to his car and peeled out, following close behind. In quick succession the other vehicles in the caravan joined him.

Meanwhile, the Cadillac sped south on Koval Lane, followed by the panicked ladies in the Sebring, who were blindly trying to get as far from the shooting as fast as possible. They didn't succeed. After a few hundred feet, more gunfire erupted from the fleeing Caddy.

The Sebring screeched to a halt as, half a block ahead of them, the assailants disappeared down a side street.

In the BMW, a panicked and bleeding Suge made a wide wobbling turn onto Las Vegas Boulevard, doing his best to avoid the heavy traffic before eventually colliding with the concrete meridian, riding up on the deflated front tire and blowing out the other in the process. "You hit?" asked Suge.

"I'm hit," Tupac replied, his voice stricken and faint.

A moment later police on bicycles arrived alongside the stalled vehicle. Among them was Officer Paul Ehler, who had radioed ahead for additional support and an ambulance. Within minutes the scene was swarming with officers, who immediately ordered everyone in the convoy out of their cars and facedown on the sidewalk. That included Suge, whose head by now was covered with blood from his scalp and neck wounds. Tupac, on the other hand, was left alone in the front seat, obviously too gravely injured to move, his breathing shallow, passing in and out of consciousness. "Got to keep your eyes open," he muttered.

Still trying to sort out what exactly had happened and whether it was victims or perpetrators laying spread-eagled on the street in front of them, LVMPD officers finally allowed Suge and his associates to stand up just as the paramedics arrived. "I can't breathe," Tupac repeatedly told the emergency medical personnel as Suge and Alexander lifted him out of the car and placed him on the ground. The response team opened a gurney and wheeled Tupac's limp body into the ambulance. With the injured Suge taking a seat inside, it sped off with sirens blaring, heading for University Medical Center, some three miles away. There, Tupac was rushed into surgery, doctors working desperately to try to stabilize his quickly deteriorating condition. It would be the first of several surgeries Tupac would endure as an ever-expanding team of physicians fought to save his life.

Placed on a ventilator and a respirator, Tupac was put into a drug-induced coma while friends and family gathered for a twenty-four-hour bedside vigil. His mother, Afeni Shakur, received the grim news in the Stone Mountain, Georgia, home that her son had purchased for her. She arrived the next morning, accompanied by family members. Joining them in what had clearly become a deathwatch was, among others, Mike Tyson, the Reverend Al Sharpton, and the entertainer MC Hammer, who arrived at the hospital in a Hummer.

Suge Knight also took his turn at the bedside of the comatose Tupac. His wounds had turned out to be superficial, but he had other problems to deal with. As a convicted felon he had been required to register with the local authorities within twenty-four hours of his arrival. Even as Tupac was struggling for breath, Suge was being fingerprinted and photographed, his presence in Las Vegas duly noted in Nevada's convicted-felon registry.

There was another unlikely visitor at University Medical Center in the hours immediately following the shooting. It was Kevin Hackie, the one-time Compton School Police Department officer who had been Russell Poole's primary source in fingering the rogue Rampart officers as Death Row operatives. He had since gone on to work at Wright Way security and had been present at the drive-by on Flamingo Road. Materializing outside the Intensive Care Unit, he had identified himself as an FBI agent investigating the shooting. Hackie did indeed have a link to the agency, but it was hardly what he claimed. In 1996 he had offered himself as an informant to the Bureau, an aspiration that had apparently gone to his head. "There is concern that Hackie is prone to exaggeration and is unstable," his FBI handler later wrote in a telling understatement. Hackie himself would later confirm his unstable state when, during a subsequent court proceeding, he told an attorney, "I am stressed out and have been on medication for the past five years. My memory is bad. I probably won't even remember our conversation tomorrow." Given his admitted condition, it is perhaps not surprising that the onetime school cop was now attempting an impersonation in an attempt to take charge of the high-profile murder case.

It was all part of a circus atmosphere ramping up even as Tupac's life ebbed away. Jesse Jackson, for example, was front and center in the media whirlwind that had descended as the news spread, busily and visibly organizing a prayer vigil in churches around the city. "Sometimes the lure of violent culture is so magnetic that even when one overcomes it with material success, it continues to call," he intoned. "We need to understand and know about the background of this man and where he came from." It was an abrupt about-face for Jackson, who had once vehemently denounced gangsta rap from the pulpit.

Wherever Tupac had come from, it was clear enough where he was heading. While refusing to speculate on his chances for survival, the head of the hospital's trauma unit let slip that only one in five patients who had sustained such wounds was likely to recover. "It's a very fatal injury," he told reporters. "Statistically, it carries a very high mortality rate. A patient may die from lack of oxygen or may bleed to death in the chest."

In a last-ditch attempt to stanch the internal hemorrhaging, doctors removed Tupac's right lung. Shortly afterward his heart failed. Physicians were able to get it pumping, only to have it give out again. It was at that point that Tupac's mother intervened, making the agonizing decision that, if his heart stopped a third time, the doctors should make no further attempts to revive him.

"I felt it was really important for Tupac," Afeni Shakur later explained on ABC's *Prime Time Live*, "who fought so hard to have a free spirit...I rejoiced with him, with the release of his spirit."

On Friday, September 13, 1996, six frantic days after the drive-by, Tupac's spirit was indeed released as he succumbed at last to his insuperable wounds. But it was hardly the act of closure that his mother might have hoped for. By his death, Shakur had become a legend, one that grew to take on a life of its own in the years that followed. It was a myth wrapped in a mystery, gripping the public imagination by posing more questions than it could ever hope to answer.

CHAPTER 15

"That Wasn't Us"

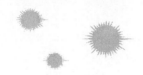

THERE WAS A GRIM SYMMETRY to the murders of Tupac Shakur and Biggie Smalls, an echo chamber amplifying the cross talk of conspiracy, which had lost none of its persuasive power over the years.

It was hard *not* to draw a direct link: both victims were huge stars, at the height of their appeal, with long and lucrative careers in front of them. Both had been at the forefront of a street-level musical revolution, one that had taken the world by storm, celebrated and condemned in equal measure. Both had been killed by semiautomatic gunfire sprayed from the window of a passing car. And both, ultimately, were seen as martyrs of the gang wars that had engulfed rap music in bloody and pointless turf battles, a conflict that their own talents had helped to foster and fuel.

As with any celebrity gone before their time, the intertwined deaths of Biggie and Tupac had become the subject of rampant speculation, including the inevitable rumors that they had, in fact, actually survived the assassination attempts. Tales were told of Biggie hiding out in Compton, having taken on the alias of Guerilla Black, who turned out to be a South Side rapper bearing a striking resemblance to Wallace that he was not shy about exploiting. Tupac was supposedly spotted in 2009, drinking hand grenades in a New Orleans bar. Chuck D, of the pioneering hip-hop group Public Enemy, became one of the more vocal conspiracy theorists. He pointed out that, among other suspicious occurrences, no pictures had been taken of Tupac in the hospital and that, on the cover of *The Don Killuminati*, he appeared in the guise of Jesus Christ, suggesting, for anyone with eyes to see, an imminent return.

It was only natural that those who mourned the loss of Tupac and Biggie would hang on to the hope of resurrection, all the more so since the circumstances of their deaths had for so long remained unresolved. Yet one factor of the twin tragedies remained demonstrably true: Tupac and Biggie were worth as much dead as alive… perhaps even more. Beginning the year after his murder, no fewer than five posthumous Tupac albums would be released on Amaru Entertainment, the label his mother started. They included *RU Still Down (Remember Me)*, which sold four million copies, and *Until the End of Time*, which racked up sales in excess of five million.

Puffy Combs was only slightly less industrious in capitalizing on the legacy of Bad Boy's fallen hero. In the summer of 1997, Combs released his own solo album, the Grammy Award-winning *No Way Out*, featuring Biggie rapping on five tracks. Two years later, Combs came out with *Born Again*, a collection of previously unreleased Biggie material grafted onto newly recorded duet tracks with Missy Elliot, Ice Cube, and Snoop Dogg. The album sold three million copies. In 2005, Combs repeated the concept on *Duets: The Final Chapter*, featuring vocal pairings with Eminem and Biggie's former wife, Faith Evans. It was followed in 2009 by the well-received biopic *Notorious*, co-produced by Combs and Biggie's mother.

One aspect of Biggie's legacy that Combs seemed to steer well clear of, however, was the murder itself. According to an article in *Rolling Stone*, the music mogul not only proved less than fully cooperative in the homicide investigation, but also appeared to discourage others from assisting in the inquiries. The magazine cited Eugene Deal's claim that, after Puffy learned the bodyguard had spoken to police, Combs refused to hire him again. Gregory Young is also quoted, asserting that Combs had warned him and others, "if our names even appear on a witness list, we're out of a job." Voletta Wallace, Biggie's mother, also weighed in on rumors of Puffy's intimidating tactics. "If Puffy has been threatening people with the loss of their jobs for cooperating with the police," she told *Rolling Stone*, "I want that made public."

As the appeal of Biggie and Tupac endured, so too did the belief in a connection between the two shootings. As the task force entered its third year of intensive investigation, we had become increasingly convinced that the trail we were following would sooner or later merge the tragedy on Flamingo Road with the one on Wilshire Boulevard. Yet the stubborn question remained: what exactly *was* the link? In many ways, we had been groping for that answer from the very first day of the reopened investigation. It had been a long, slow, and frustrating process, with more than its share of dead ends. Tray Lane, Corey Edwards, Michael Dorrough: each had led into a blind alley, and we were no closer to untangling the puzzle than when we'd begun. We hoped our luck would change when Keffe D finally started opening up.

It was that air of expectancy that hung over the conference room in Wayne Higgins's office on the morning of December 18, 2008, when Daryn and I, joined again by Bill Holcomb and Jeff Bennett, sat down for our first follow-up meeting with Keffe D. We had come to hear what he had promised would blow our "fuckin' minds." It was a tantalizing prospect. At the same time, we couldn't help but wonder how useful his story would turn out to be. As he had whispered to me in the hallway prior to our initial sit-down, he didn't "know nothin' about what you want to talk to me for." As we had told Wayne Higgins, what we wanted to talk to him for was concrete information about the Biggie Smalls homicide. Was that now off the table?

Years of experience had taught me that detective work is as much about improvisation as it is about investigation. We had worked long and hard to compel Keffe D's cooperation. What form that cooperation took, and what direction it might lead, was something we couldn't foresee. We had to go where he took us.

After some pleasantries, we cut to the chase. Did he know anything about the Biggie Smalls murder? He just shrugged. "I already told you," he said. "That one wasn't us." Daryn and I looked at each other. Were we reading the same thing between the same lines? If Davis was denying complicity in "that one," was there another one that, by implication, he *was* involved in?

When Keffe D shrugged his shoulders it was like lifting the heavy burden of a man who knew too much about too many things. He stared at us with his heavy-lidded eyes.

"What can you tell us about this deal?" Daryn persisted.

A moment passed. Then another. "I saw Puffy at the House of Blues the night before it went down," he answered at last. "He told me to come out for the big ball game at the school."

We knew immediately what he was referring to: the celebrity basketball match that Biggie, along with Lil' Caesar and the Bad Boy security head, Paul Offord, had attended at Cal State Dominguez Hills on the day of the Petersen party. Just the fact that Combs had invited him to the event told us something. Keffe D was still seemingly in the good graces of the music mogul he had first met by providing a Crip security contingent for the West Coast leg of a Bad Boy concert tour in 1995.

"Who else was at the game?" I asked.

"Snoop Dogg. Kurupt," he answered, naming two prominent Death Row artists, who despite their association with Suge's label were Crip-affiliated. It was for that reason, Keffe D claimed, that he gave them a "pass."

"Who else?" Daryn pressed.

"Puffy. Biggie." After the game, he told us, Keffe D received invitations to the Vibe event and that evening he arrived at the Petersen in the company of his nephew Baby Lane, Dre Smith and other major South Side Crips.

Inside the museum, Keffe D spotted Biggie and Puffy around their ringside table at the dance floor. He approached them and was waved through security by Combs. "Puff seemed all nervous," he continued. "He said the feds were all over him and he didn't want me to catch his heat." We wondered at first if he was referring to the ongoing investigation out of Teaneck, looking into narcotics and weapons allegations against Biggie and that, perhaps, Puffy felt himself to be a target as well. But as we listened, Daryn and I couldn't help but wonder if Puffy wasn't just trying to distance himself from a gangster of Keffe D's stature. As his star rose, the music mogul had less and less reason to associate himself with hardcore gangbangers and we had no reason to believe that the "heat" in Keffe D's account was actually generated by the New Jersey investigation or was simply a figment of Puffy's imagination.

Biggie, on the other hand, seemed to have thrown caution entirely to the wind, at one point interrupting the conversation to ask if Keffe D had any "chronic" he'd be willing to trade for a bottle of Cristal champagne.

Yet, for his part, Keefe D remained alert to potential trouble, if not from federal authorities then from the various gang factions that thronged the Petersen's Grand Salon. "There were a lot of Blood motherfuckers there," he told us, "and Death Row, too. DJ Quik and two singers named Jewell and Lashelle, who was Suge's cousin and had been signed by him. I told Puffy to watch his ass, but he didn't pay no mind. He told me the two bitches had come to New York to see him about being on Bad Boy 'cause they was tired of working in Suge's stable."

Keffe D was skeptical. He knew that Jewell, an aspiring R&B vocalist, had strong links to Death Row and posed a potential threat. She had shot her live-in boyfriend in 1993 and had subsequently been arrested for helping to launder millions in a drug operation. Neither charge stuck. When asked by investigators in that case what her connection to Death Row was, she replied only that she had provided services, whatever that meant. Keffe D apparently suspected that the service Jewell was providing that night was as an operative for Suge, casing the Petersen party.

Moments before the fire marshal announced that the party was being shut down, Keffe D claimed that Puffy had asked to meet them back at the hotel. "I was fixin' to leave after that," he continued, "when I got told that Biggie was shot."

"Who did it?" I asked, seeing no harm in reiterating the obvious question.

Keffe D gave me an impatient look. "I told you," he repeated. "That wasn't us." There was silence around the table. It was clear that we had gone as far as we were going to go on the subject of the Wallace homicide.

The implications of Keffe D's statement seemed clear to us. If he had nothing to say about Biggie, then he *had* to be talking about Tupac. He had been present at both murders and it was the only part of his story that would be remotely mind-blowing enough. The task facing us at that point was to determine if he was telling the truth or simply stringing us along.

I reached into my briefcase and produced the statements Keffe D had made to the FBI in prison after his arrest in 1997 on federal drug charges. In it, he had given his version of what happened in Las

Vegas the night Tupac was killed, claiming that he had driven to the city on the day of the boxing match in the company of his brother Kevin, Cory Edwards, and other assorted Crips, including Terrence "Bubble Up" Brown.

After checking in to the MGM Grand Hotel, Keffe D continued, the crew had purchased tickets for the fight from a scalper. After the match, they had all gone to a restaurant where an associate informed Keefe D of the beating his nephew had received from Tupac and his Death Row enforcers. Baby Lane, Keffe D had told agents, arrived earlier in the day, driving out separately in a rented Cadillac. His companions on the trip were fellow Crips, Terrence Brown, who had been convicted of numerous felonies, and Dre Smith, who would be dead in a few years from complications due to morbid obesity. The trio checked into the Excalibur Hotel.

Subsequently meeting up with his bruised and mortified nephew, Keffe D claimed to have counseled caution. Revenge would have to wait, he supposedly told Baby Lane. There were too many cops beefing up security for the championship bout. They could settle the score once they got back to Compton. But they never got the chance. Somebody beat them to it.

Baby Lane had every reason to want Tupac and Suge dead, the FBI interviewer persisted. If he didn't do it, who did?

Keffe D denied any knowledge of the killer's identity. When asked by the agent to speculate, he suggested with a straight face that Compton police officers, hired by Suge, had done the deed. When pressed as to what possible motive Suge might have for killing his star client, and putting himself in the line of fire, Keffe D theorized that Tupac had threatened to leave Death Row Records and Suge hired the cops to kill him for his disloyalty.

As ridiculous on its face as such a reason might have seemed, it had gained considerable traction in the years since Tupac's death. Produced in 1997 by Tupac's Las Vegas bodyguard, Frank Alexander, a DVD documentary titled *Tupac: Assassination* went to great lengths to make the same case, falling well short of producing much credible evidence. Not that it made a difference. That was Keffe D's story, the one he had stuck to for almost ten years.

We waited as the gangster finished perusing the statement he had made behind bars to federal authorities. As he turned over the last page, he threw us all a scornful look. "That's all bullshit," he said.

It was as if, in that moment, we could feel the ice finally beginning to break apart, freeing the long frozen case. Keffe D had admitted that the tale he'd spun for the FBI was a lie, which meant that there must be another story. One that might actually be true.

CHAPTER 16

"Was That Us?"

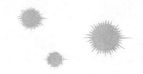

TWO WEEKS LATER, with the morning sun streaming through the wide conference room windows, we met with Keffe D again. Higgins's law firm had recently moved into the vacated Death Row Records headquarters and it wasn't hard to imagine that this same space might have been the infamous Red Room where Suge Knight held court.

This time around, the one and only topic up for discussion was the murder of Tupac, which, by process of elimination, we had concluded had been Keffe D's bargaining chip all along. We asked him to take it from the top, knowing full well how difficult it is to find the starting point in any gang narrative. Aside from the famously permeable nature of memory, which sometimes accounts for the wide divergences in eyewitness testimony, the exploits of gangsters often bleed into one another, sometimes literally. Characters and events overlap as friends and enemies regularly swap places backward and forward through time. It was up to us to sort through it all.

Sure enough, Keefe D began his story in 1991, "back in the day," when the South Side Crips would play weekend baseball with the Santana Block crew in a Compton park, the winners taking home a case of Dom Perignon. It was at a time when the Crips were consolidating their national drug distribution networks, and at one of these games, Keffe D told us, that he had been introduced to a New York-based dealer named Eric "Zip" Martin, also known as Equan Williams.

Zip operated a Manhattan limousine service and a Harlem nightclub called Zip Code. According to Keffe D, he made frequent trips to Los Angeles to find suppliers for a thriving East Coast drug business with Keefe D eventually furnishing kilos of cocaine to Martin. He told us that at one point he flew out and stayed in Zip's Jersey City apartment while making arrangements for the transport of large quantities of PCP from Compton.

Two years later, our witness continued, Zip was back in Los Angeles and invited his business partner along for a Black Entertainment Television function at the Paradise Club, a trendy Westside nightspot. According to Keffe D, Zip had carefully cultivated connections in the music industry, and it was there that he first introduced Keffe D to Puffy Combs. On the verge of launching his Bad Boy entertainment empire, Puffy had already been credited with discovering the superstar diva Mary J. Blige, who also made an appearance at the event.

Keefe D claimed that he had quickly put himself in Puffy's good graces when he supposedly lent out his vintage 1964 Chevy LS for the music video of "Can U Get with It," the debut single by a young vocalist named Usher, who Combs was producing. Such a vehicle does indeed appear in the video, driven by Puffy himself and when the vehicle was damaged during the filming, Keffe D asserted, Combs made sure he was reimbursed for the $2,500 repair bill.

Keffe D insisted that their relationship flourished as Puffy's growing fame increasingly brought him to Los Angeles. He asserted that, while in town, Combs met with him on several occasions at Greenblatt's Deli, a famous eatery on Sunset Boulevard adjacent to the Laugh Factory comedy club. There, over corned beef and coleslaw lunches, the topic of conversation, as recounted by Keefe D, became increasingly focused on the rivalry between the East and West Coast rap factions. After the Quad Studios ambush, Tupac had not been shy in publicly declaring that Puffy had orchestrated the attack. Suge Knight would level similar accusations against Combs regarding the death of his friend and bodyguard Jake Robles in an Atlanta nightclub.

But the feud had really escalated when Suge appeared on a New York stage during an awards show sponsored by *The Source* magazine. In a cutting reference to Puffy's spotlight-grabbing tendency, Suge had told the crowd, "Any hip-hop artists out there who want to be an artist and stay a star, and don't want to have to worry about the executive producer trying to be all in the videos, and on all the records...come to Death Row."

Not long afterward, Keffe D continued, he and Zip were driving through Compton together when Martin's cell phone rang. It was Puffy, and he wanted to speak to Keffe D. "He was like, 'Man, you think it's cool to come out there for our concerts?'" Keefe D recounted to us. "I'm talking about Big Boy—the CEO." The reference was clearly to Suge Knight and Keffe D knew it immediately. "I told him, 'That boy ain't nothing. Come on, we got your back...just give me about forty-five or fifty tickets.'"

It was a story supported by a statement we would subsequently take from Denvonta Lee, who told us that he had witnessed Keffe D passing out concert tickets to Bad Boy Entertainment events. For that reason, he assumed, the comps had come from Combs.

To our ears, the twin account had the ring of truth. We believed that Puffy had used Crips as security for the Southern California leg of his 1995 Summer Jam tour. And if Keefe D was to be believed, it was a fistful of tickets that had paid for their services.

Given Puffy's unequivocal denial that he had ever compensated Crips for security, there is inevitably an element of ambiguity in the conflicting accounts. Could handing out freebees be considered payment for protection? In short, did Puffy "hire" a Crip posse?

It seemed to be a distinction without a difference in Keffe D's mind. "He gave us the tickets and I brought the crew," he told us. "That's when we brought out the forces...we went up there deep."

According to Keefe D's story, he and a large contingent of Crips had gathered in Combs' hotel suite prior to the Anaheim concert. Aside from his regular security team and the gang contingent, Puffy allegedly told Keefe D that he had several trained Navy SEALs as backup in an adjacent room.

"Was he worried about something happening?" Daryn asked.

"He was scared to death," Keffe D retorted. "That's when he said it in front of all these people...he said he'd give anything for them dudes' heads."

Daryn and I looked at each other. Had we just heard what we thought we heard? Was Keffe D saying that Puffy Combs had made a solicitation for the murder of Suge Knight and Tupac Shakur?

"Who was there that day?" I asked.

"At Anaheim?" Keffe D replied. "Everybody. The whole fuckin' neighborhood."

I leaned forward. "Give us five names of people who would say, 'Yeah, we heard Puffy say that.'"

He identified Michael "Owl" Dorrough, Corey Edwards, and Dirt Rock as present at the scene. "All of them will tell you," he insisted. "He said it in front of all them people. I couldn't believe it. A whole room full of Crips."

"Tell us what happened," I pressed, "that made it something other than him just frustrated and boasting? What made it specific, like, 'Hey, I'm serious, I want you guys to kill these guys.'"

"When he told me at Greenblatt's," Keffe D answered promptly. He went on to describe an alleged encounter at the delicatessen during which Puffy had pulled him aside. "He was like, 'I want to get rid of them dudes.'" When Daryn asked him whether Puffy always referred to Suge and Tupac together, Keffe D nodded, adding that Tupac had been added to the hit list "after he made that record."

"After 'Hit 'Em Up,' came out," Daryn specified, referring to the 1996 single on which Tupac had called out Puffy and Biggie by name.

"Yeah," Keffe D answered. "That pissed him off…I was like, 'Man, we'll wipe their ass out, quick…it's nothing. Consider that done.' We wanted a million dollars."

"Who brought up the amount?" Holcomb asked.

"He did….shit, a million. I'd take fifty thousand."

"So you tell him you'll do it for million," I repeated, "and he's like 'OK.' He agrees. You shake on it or something like that?"

"No. It was more like a gentlemen's…" He stopped, searching for the term. "Know what I'm saying?"

We knew what he was saying, all right. We were just having a hard time staying ahead of it all. According to Keffe D, Puffy Combs had put out a million-dollar contract on Suge Knight and Tupac Shakur. Which begged the next question.

"OK," I said slowly. "So you guys make the deal." Did they go out to Las Vegas to make good on it?

Keffe D shook his head vehemently. "We didn't even have any pistols," he insisted. He and his posse were just there for the fight. They had, he claimed, left for the Tyson-Seldon match that afternoon after breakfast at Gleenblatt's, Zip in a Mercedes, Keffe D driving a rented Buick Century, and his brother Kevin Davis following in a rented van with a group of gang associates.

Up to this point Keffe D's story tracked closely with the account he had given to the FBI in 1998. Baby Lane Anderson, he told us, had arrived the following day with Dre Smith and Terrence "Bubble Up" Brown, in a rented Cadillac. Keffe D and Zip had gotten tickets to the fight from a scalper and had gone out to dinner following the bout. It was there that Keffe D first got word that his nephew, who he hadn't seen since his arrival, had been roughed up by Tupac, Suge, and the Mob Piru enforcers in the lobby of the MGM Grand.

But it was at this juncture that Keffe D suddenly dropped the old story and provided us a startlingly different version. Far from advising Baby Lane to bide his time until they returned to Compton, Keffe D claimed that he, his nephew and the others immediately began planning a counterattack. Zip arrived to offer assistance, he continued, and together they walked to the hotel parking lot. It was there, in a bizarre cameo, that the rapper Foxy Brown sat waiting in Zip's Benz. Six months later, of course, she would be outside the Petersen on the night Biggie was killed.

According to Keffe D, after ejecting Foxy, Zip opened the armrest compartment and produced a .40-caliber Glock handgun. "He said it's perfect timing," Keefe D recounted, leaving the exact meaning of the words up to us. Was Zip talking about killing two birds with one stone, taking out Suge and Tupac as payback for the Baby Lane beating and in the process collecting Puffy's million-dollar bounty? It was impossible to know for sure, since, in Keefe D's account, Zip departed shortly afterwards, leaving the others to carry out the job by themselves.

Meanwhile, news of Tupac and Suge's scheduled appearance at Club 662 had spread quickly. With that destination in mind, Keefe D said, the crew assembled at the MGM Grand entrance. He and Kevin Davis got into the rental van with the Crips Wendell Prince, Corey Edwards, and Tracy Sessions, along with another passenger, said to be from Detroit and unknown to Keffe D. They headed down

Las Vegas Boulevard, his story continued, followed by the Cadillac carrying Baby Lane, Terrence Brown, and Deandre Smith. Forty-five minutes later, fighting the same heavy traffic that had slowed down the Death Row caravan, they pulled into the parking lot of the club.

The nightspot was crowded with fans in anticipation of Tupac's arrival and the group of nine men did their best to blend in with the excited fans. But, according to Keffe D, the anticipation proved too much and a few of them, most especially Corey Edwards, began to lose their nerve. After twenty minutes they left, driving to a nearby liquor store for some liquid courage. It was then, said Keffe D, that he joined Orlando, Dre and Brown in the Cadillac. Leaving the others in the van at the parking lot, they drove back toward the club in the Caddy. Brown was behind the wheel, with Keffe D next to him in the front passenger seat, carrying Zip's Glock. Dre occupied the rear seat behind the driver, with Orlando next to him.

"We came up to Las Vegas Boulevard," Keefe D recounted, "and here he come in the BMW, the broads going 'Tupac! Tupac!' He gave himself away. So we made a U-turn and pulled up on the side and checked every car to see where he was."

As the caravan turned down Flamingo Road and stopped for the light at Koval Lane, the Caddy moved up until it was parallel with the 750. "I thought we was going to pull up on my side," Keffe D continued.

"So you were fixing to blast if you had to?" I asked.

"If we would have been on my side, I would've blasted."

"So you handed the gun to the backseat?"

"Yeah, I gave it to Dre but he was like 'No, no, no,' and Lane was like 'Give it here' and popped the dude."

Thirteen shots later, Brown accelerated into a hard right turn, followed by Ingrid Johnson and her girlfriends in the Sebring. "Stupid bitches," Keffe D remarked, recalling that the women finally pulled to a stop. The Caddy drove into a parking lot across from the Carriage

House, a hotel on East Harmon Avenue. Scrambling from the vehicle, Keffe D stated, Orlando hid the Glock in the right front wheel well of the Caddy. They then continued on foot back toward the Monte Carlo Hotel, where Keffe D was staying. As they headed to the casino entrance, they heard sirens wailing down the Strip and a moment later the ambulance carrying Tupac and the wounded Suge passed them by. "The ambulance was right next to us," Keefe D remembered. "That shit was as funny as a motherfucker."

Shortly after they arrived at the hotel, the remainder of the crew left behind in the van at the liquor store arrived. "They didn't even know we did it," Keffe D asserted. "I didn't tell nobody shit." Instead they went up to his room to "smoke weed and drink."

The next morning, he continued, Brown went back to the Cadillac to pick up any stray shell casings and dispose of the murder weapon. Keffe D, his wife, Paula, along with Baby Lane and his girlfriend, returned to Los Angeles. The following day, claimed Keffe D, he received a phone call from Zip, requesting a meeting at a Hollywood hot wings stand at the corner of Melrose and La Brea. Puffy had called, Keffe D asserted that Zip had told him. He wanted to know, "Was that us?'"

"Did you talk to Puff, too?" Holcomb asked. Keefe D nodded, telling us that Combs had called again during his meeting with Zip.

"So," Jeff Bennett asked, "when you talk to Puff on the phone does he ask you, 'Was that us?'"

"Yeah," Keffe D replied. "He was happy as hell."

"Did you ask him about the money?" Daryn interjected. "About when you were going to get paid?"

"No. I told Zip to go get our cash."

"So Zip was going to handle that part?" Daryn pressed.

"Yeah. I kept calling his ass." Finally, after six weeks of trying, Keefe D told us, he arranged a meeting with Zip at the Roxbury, a music-business watering hole on Sunset Boulevard. It was there that

Zip told him, "Puffy ain't gave it to me yet." Keffe D was soon to hear otherwise, when a rumor reached him from, among others, Combs associate Darrius "D Mack" Rodgers, that Puffy might have actually paid Zip for the murders. But by then there was little he could do to collect. He had been arrested in a major federal narcotics sweep.

We paused, looking at one another, trying to get our heads around what we had just heard. A long moment passed. Finally I turned back to Keffe D. "Since you've been out of prison," I asked, "have you talked to Zip?"

"Not one time."

"What about Puffy?"

"Not one time," he repeated. "I tried to call him several times, though…if he would have just given us half the money, I would have stayed strong."

There was no reason to ask why Keffe D would have settled for half the contract fee. Tupac was dead. Suge was still alive. Only half the job had been done.

PART
FIVE

CHAPTER 17

"Cleared Other"

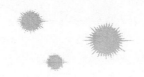

IN DETECTIVE WORK what you look for so long and hard is often what's been staring you in the face the whole time. As a rule, a criminal investigation is nothing like a whodunit: there's rarely some last-minute revelation that it's the last person you expected. Usually, it's the suspect that was right up front with the means, motive and opportunity. The simple fact is that investigations aren't primarily about solving a mystery. They're about proving the facts.

We now had evidence that pointed to Orlando "Baby Lane" Anderson as the killer of Tupac Shakur. With the benefit of hindsight it seemed obvious. If, prior to our interviews with Keffe D in late 2008, I'd been asked to put together a list of the most likely suspects, he'd have been at the top of the list. Knowing that didn't make us great detectives. It was just common sense.

Anyone who had spent any time looking into the murder of Tupac Shakur had a pretty good idea who was responsible. That was especially true in Baby Lane's Compton neighborhood. According to Keffe D's statements, the women who had accompanied the Crips contingent out to Las Vegas, including his wife, Paula, were soon talking openly about what had gone down and who had pulled the trigger. It was just the kind of notoriety a gangster thrived on, even though, when directly confronted by investigative reporters, Baby Lane would indignantly deny everything. "If they have all this evidence against me," he was quoted as saying nearly a year after the event, "then why haven't they arrested me? It's obvious that I'm innocent."

What was obvious, of course, was something very different. But absent an inside account, it was impossible to prove. With Keffe D's story we felt we had the proof we needed. He had put himself in the Cadillac, willing, as he had told us, to do the job himself if they had only pulled up on the other side of the BMW carrying Suge and Tupac.

To those of us in the task force, it made little difference that the suspect we had for so long sought had been dead for more than a decade. Our job was to close the case. And there was more than one way to do that. In the LAPD's *Detective Operations Manual* the option is spelled out in the definition of the term "Cleared Other." "When a crime report is...'Cleared Other,'" the manual reads, "it means that the detective has solved the crime and has taken all possible, appropriate action against at least one suspect. It also means that no further action or investigation is expected to take place regarding the suspect...'Cleared Other' shall be indicated when a case has progressed to a point where further action cannot reasonably be taken." In a subsection delineating how a case is declared "Cleared Other," the first item on a list of circumstances of being "outside of police control" is "death of the perpetrator."

It would have been nice to make a headlining arrest of Tupac Shakur's murderer, bring Baby Lane in for a perp walk and claim our fifteen minutes of fame. But that wasn't going to happen. "Cleared Other" was as close as we were going to get and, as far as we were concerned, that was close enough, especially when it came to an investigation that had languished in a cold-case file for a dozen years. For the friends and family of Tupac Shakur, we had offered, at long last, a chance for closure.

Orlando certainly seemed to have a surplus of motives to gun down Tupac in cold blood. We'd never know, of course, whether he pulled the trigger to restore his stained honor after the beating at the MGM Grand; to collect on the reward which Keefe D claimed that Puffy Combs had allegedly put on the heads of his rivals; or some combination of the two. But there was no question of his reasons for abruptly switching sides when Suge Knight subsequently faced a parole violation for his part in the MGM fracas.

As Keffe D alleged in a subsequent interview, Suge had met with Baby Lane several weeks after the shooting and offered him $16,000 in exchange for testimony exonerating Knight from involvement in the beating. When, after the meeting, an angry Keffe D asked his nephew why he was cooperating with the man who had humiliated him, Baby Lane had a simple response: "For the money."

In point of fact, it seemed that Baby Lane never felt the need to explain anything he did, least of all the killing of Tupac Shakur. Like many others who had grown up on the streets of South Central Los Angeles, killing was its own reward, a reflexive reaction to slights real or imagined. The necessary proof of being a player came with an utter disregard for human life. That was the code he lived and, ultimately, died by, cut down on a Compton street corner in a hail of bullets over a trifling drug debt.

While there was still much left to do, we were confident we were closing in on the Tupac murder. But it wasn't quite that simple. For one thing, it was not technically our call to make. The crime had occurred in Las Vegas. It was up to the LVMPD to declare the case closed, "Other" or otherwise. Normal procedure would be for us to turn over the results of our investigation to them—except that there was nothing normal about this case. What our work had uncovered went far beyond territorial protocol. If Keffe D was to be believed, Tupac's death was the result of a murder-for-hire conspiracy initiated by Puffy Combs around a delicatessen table well within the LAPD's jurisdiction. The alleged plot to kill the rapper had unfolded in our backyard and, as such, we could justifiably claim control over that part of the case.

But it was a slippery slope and we knew it. Strictly speaking, Vegas had a prior claim on Keffe D's explosive allegations. But what would they do with it if we gave it to them? We were apprehensive that the Las Vegas investigators would insist on conducting their own interviews with various Persons of Interest, potentially exposing Keffe D as our source and impairing his ability to further assist us in the investigation.

We couldn't let that happen. For one thing, there was a lot more we wanted to ask him. Detectives had lined up as soon as they heard about our talkative witness, eager to grill him on any number of unsolved cases. But more important, *we* weren't finished with him. Finding out who had pulled the trigger on Tupac was just the first step. The next move was to gather evidence that would support Keefe D's claim that Puffy Combs had initiated the hit. And for that we needed his continuing cooperation.

Of course, making the decision to deny police in another jurisdiction information that would have a direct bearing on an investigation they were still, at least in theory, conducting was way above our pay grade. Accordingly, during the mandatory monthly briefing with Chief William Bratton, we conferred with LAPD chief legal council Gerald Chaleff. One of the city's more renowned defense attorneys, Chaleff had been named the department's lead legal advisor after serving as president of the civilian Board of Police Commissioners, where he oversaw the Consent Decree Bureau, the Risk Management Group, and the Civil Rights Integrity Division.

In short, Chaleff knew better than anyone the lines of authority and accountability within law enforcement jurisdictions. He could be depended upon to accurately assess the risks of cutting Las Vegas out of the loop. It was his decision, along with Chief Bratton, that we were not obliged to notify the LVMPD of our findings, thus freeing us to pursue the broader conspiracy case without jeopardizing our prized informant.

We were well aware of that informant's shortcomings as a credible witness in any legal proceeding. No court in the country was going to accept the word of Duane Keith "Keffe D" Davis, a convicted felon and a self-confessed liar. As to whether *we* believed what Keffe D was telling us, with certain reservations I'd have to say that we did. Granting his checkered past, and even discounting the incentive to honesty that U.S. Attorney Searight's proffer agreement had provided, it seemed unlikely that Keffe D would willingly name himself as a co-conspirator in a major homicide case unless it was true. It would have been easy enough to distance himself from the carnage on Flamingo Road if he'd wanted to hedge his bets. Instead he implicated himself in a premeditated murder, claiming to have received the murder weapon from Zip Martin and driving to Club 662 with malice aforethought. He'd even boasted that he would have done the killing himself but for an accident of fate. According to his account, Tupac might never have been shot without the impetus provided by Keffe D. It was our considered opinion that we were getting the real story from a key participant in the crime.

But we were equally certain that his story would be taken apart by a team of defense attorneys accomplished in the art of dismantling witnesses. Sean Puffy Combs, and whatever high-powered legal team he might assemble, would never allow his allegations to stand unchallenged. If we were going to make our case for murder and conspiracy we'd have to come up with compelling new evidence that substantiated what Keffe D had told us. And that wasn't going to be easy.

Of the principals allegedly involved in Tupac's murder, Keffe D's nephew, of course, was no longer available to assist in our inquiries. Nor was Dre Smith, who, against all odds, had died of natural causes brought on by morbid obesity. That left the wheelman, Terrence Brown. But for the moment, going after Brown made little sense. There was no indication that he had any knowledge of the bounty Puffy had, according to Keffe D, put on Tupac's and Suge's heads. And it was that element of the case that we were focused on. Brown could wait. That left one participant who could help us get to Puffy: Zip.

The plan, as Daryn and I formulated it in the weeks following the December meeting in Higgins's office, was essentially a repeat of the tactics we had used to bring in Keffe D, arranging for him to reestablish contact with his onetime business partner for the ostensible purpose of setting up a new narcotics network between L.A. and Zip's New York base of operations. If we could catch Zip in the act of buying drugs, we could put the squeeze on him to confirm Keffe D's claim regarding Puffy's million-dollar contract to eliminate Tupac and Suge.

The plan was not without its potential problems. For one thing, Keffe D and Zip had not seen each other since they had met in Hollywood a few days after the murder. For Keffe D to suddenly show up at Zip's doorstep might raise some disconcerting questions, especially considering the unfinished business between the two. Keffe D still firmly believed that Zip had collected on half of the bounty Puffy had put up. Zip might understandably be nervous to see his old friend turning up to collect on his cut of the money. It was imperative to move cautiously. Keffe D would have to put on a performance that would convince Zip that he neither bore a grudge nor was looking to collect on the alleged bounty. More to the point, he had to make his interest in establishing a new drug operation sound credible. It would take time to gain Zip's trust.

For his part, Keffe D seemed supremely confident in his ability to pull off the ruse. He even went so far as to suggest that he should instead go straight to Puffy Combs, eliciting the incriminating evidence straight from the horse's mouth. We were quick to pull him back. The Puffy with whom Keffe D had associated in 1996 was hardly the same Puffy who now looked down from the lofty peak of his entertainment empire. In the intervening twelve years Combs had spiraled upward from one high-profile triumph to another. Bad Boy Entertainment Worldwide included Bad Boy Records, a veritable hit music factory featuring its premier artist: Puff Daddy aka P. Diddy aka "Ciroc Obama,"as he had reportedly taken to calling himself; the clothing line Sean John; a movie production company; and a pair of chic restaurants. He had a rèsumè that included plum film and Broadway acting roles and a glamorous, if short-lived, romance with Jennifer Lopez. It all contributed to the renaissance man's estimated net worth of nearly $350 million. The likelihood of Puffy Combs getting together with Keffe D over lunch at Greenblatt's seemed exceedingly slim. We did our best to focus his attention on the matter at hand: getting reacquainted with Zip.

It wasn't until the early summer of 2009 that we were ready to make our move. On June 17, Daryn, Jim Black, and I escorted Keffe D on a flight from Los Angeles to New York. The following morning, Daryn, Jim, and I found ourselves driving down Adam Clayton Powell Boulevard approaching Martin's nightclub, Zip Code, to scope out the place before it opened. Even though we were with Daryn, both Jim and I were acutely aware of the hostile stares directed at two white guys snooping around in a black neighborhood. That night we returned to the location, followed this time by Keffe D in his own rented car. He and Daryn entered the club and asked for Zip. Informed that the owner was not on the premises, Keffe D left his cell number with instructions to have Martin give him a call.

Two days later, with still no word from Zip, we revisited the club, this time sending Keffe D in alone while we parked a few blocks away. This time we hit pay dirt. Zip arrived, in the company of a nephew known only as "Asziz," just as Keffe D was walking to the front entrance. He was greeted like a long-lost brother, with Zip professing delight at seeing his old homeboy alive and well. As related in Keffe D's subsequent debriefing, he told Zip that he was in town on a large drug deal with an associate in Queens and that while he was in the neighborhood he thought he'd drop by to see if Zip was interested in reviving their old business relationship.

In Keefe D's version of the subsequent exchange, Zip hesitated, claiming that he was battling cancer and was simply too old to be involved in such a high-risk enterprise anymore. However, Keffe D said, he did have a suggestion: Martin's nephew Asziz was just getting started in the trade and was on the lookout for a reliable PCP supplier. Maybe they could do some business together. Numbers were discussed, upward of $38,000 for a gallon of top-grade "embalming fluid," quite a bump from the $10,500 Keffe D was accustomed to charging back in Compton. He said he exchanged phone numbers with the young entrepreneur and promised to stay in touch.

We were encouraged by Keffe D's account of the meeting. While Zip would not be directly involved in the proposed transaction, he had supposedly done much to facilitate the arrangement, and we were hopeful that, once money began changing hands, he might want in on the action. We sent Keffe D back to Zip Code one more time to allay any possible suspicions with a purely social visit.

Shortly afterward we got an intriguing hit on a database search we had initiated back at task force headquarters. According to NY DEA agents, there was a possibility that "Asziz" was one Troy "Ish" Moore, who the agency suspected of being a lieutenant in Zip's alleged Harlem drug operation. It seemed plausible to us that Zip had put Keffe D on to Asziz as a test of his old partner's intentions. We were determined to supply Keffe D with whatever he needed to make good on those intentions.

CHAPTER 18

Sugar Bear

OUR WORK WITH KEFFE D had shed considerable new light on the question of who killed Tupac Shakur. But it had also served another purpose, one that brought us back at last to the original reason the task force had formed in the first place: to bring the killer of Christopher Wallace to justice.

"That wasn't us," Keffe D had decisively declared when we had asked him about the drive-by outside the Petersen Museum. It was, to our ears, a convincing denial. Claiming culpability in the Tupac murder lent weight to his assertion of innocence in Biggie's death. We were inclined to take him at his word, and that inclination resulted in narrowing the scope of our investigation. *Menace II Society*," the part of the case that dealt strictly with possible Crips involvement in the Biggie killing, was moving toward resolution, if Keffe D's statement was to be believed. Whatever else they might be held accountable for—including the death of Tupac—it seemed likely that the gang had had nothing to do with the Wallace murder.

That left *"Rap It Up,"* our name for the Mob Piru segment of the investigation. According to his uncle, Baby Lane, a Crip from the cradle, had killed Tupac and almost killed Suge. If that were true, then it was certainly plausible that the Piru would strike back by taking out Wallace, the biggest star in the stable of Puffy Combs. It was as simple as that.

Except that it wasn't. While we had potentially removed the Crips from our list of likely suspects in the Biggie homicide, proving that the Mob Piru was behind the hit was another matter entirely. *"Rap It Up"* was, in short, a long way from being wrapped up.

With the focus now on one gang, we had no trouble selecting a target for the next phase of our investigation: the Death Row Records founder and major Mob Piru figure, Marion "Suge" Knight. In point of fact, our attention had been turned on Suge since the inception of the task force, seeking evidence that might tie him to that bloody night at the Petersen.

His history gave us plenty to go on. Aside from his life-long law-breaking habits Suge had a certain genius for self-promotion and a gift for spotting talent, both creative and criminal, which made him that much more menacing and genuinely dangerous. A Compton native with real athletic prowess, the burly Knight was known in the neighbor-hood as Sugar Bear, eventually shortened to "Suge." By all accounts a promising student, he earned a football scholarship to the University of Nevada, where he played defense. He was recruited to the Los Angeles Rams as a replacement player during the 1987 NFL strike. But Suge's athletic ambitions proved to be a passing phase. What interested him infinitely more was the burgeoning world of hip-hop music, which by the late eighties was exploding with the advent of hardcore rap. Suge worked briefly as a concert promoter and, thanks to his hulking stature, a bodyguard for, among others, the singer Bobby Brown.

He also evinced a talent for getting into trouble. Shortly after his stint with the Rams he was brought in on a variety of charges, including auto theft, carrying a concealed weapon, and attempted murder. From 1987 to 1995 his criminal record included guilty pleas to two counts of battery; a conviction for assault with a deadly weapon; a guilty plea on two counts of assault with a firearm and repeated parole and probation violations. All the while he was demonstrating a flair for combining his criminal activity with his other ruling passion: music. In one of the earliest forays into the recording industry, he supposedly dangled the white rapper Vanilla Ice from the balcony of a twenty-story building in an effort to convince him to sign over the royalties to his smash hit, "Ice Ice Baby."

Another story tells of coaxing Easy-E and his manager, Jerry Heller, into releasing Dr. Dre from his Ruthless Records contract with a hot crack pipe and a baseball bat. Not long afterward two fledgling rappers got on Suge's bad side when they used a recording studio telephone without permission and were stripped naked and pistol-whipped. The tall tales may or may not have been true but they served their purpose: to inspire fear in the hearts of Suge Knight's rivals.

His success in launching Death Row Records with Dr. Dre is a matter of record: a lot of records. Securing a distribution deal with Interscope Records, Suge presided over one of the most successful start-up labels in recording history, thanks primarily to Dre's trademark musical gifts. But even as Suge gained respect and riches as an canny entrepreneur, his gangster antics continued apace. He staffed the company's offices with Bloods, bragging that he was giving society's outcasts a second chance. And, as he later would do with Puffy Combs and Bad Boy Records, he picked a very public fight with Luther Campbell of the Miami rap group 2 Live Crew, showing up at a 1993 hip-hop convention to confront him with a stolen gun. His most notable achievement, however, was signing Tupac Shakur, the crown jewel of his Death Row roster, using a subtle mix of diplomacy, legal aid and financial incentives. And, like his superstar acquisition, Suge had also unknowingly reached the apex of his career in Las Vegas that September night of 1996. Subsequently arrested for a parole violation in the wake of the MGM Grand incident, Suge, despite Baby Lane's suborned testimony, was given a stiff nine-year sentence.

Released in 2001, he was back in jail two years later, once again having violated the conditions of his parole. There, he watched help-lessly as his Death Row empire crumbled away, assailed by numer-ous disgruntled investors and deserted by its one time all-star roster, including Snoop Dogg. "I never was afraid of him," the rapper boasted to *Rolling Stone* magazine. "I was afraid I was gonna have to kill him. That's what I was afraid of."

Others had good reason to fear for their own lives. Many of Suge's inner circle were being picked off with careful deliberation in a sharp escalation of the running feud triggered by Tupac's murder. The fact that there were sometimes long gaps between the hits, sometimes stretching into years, only made the dread among his associates more palpable.

In the summer of 1997, less than a year after Tupac's murder, Aaron "Heron" Palmer, one of Suge's most trusted bodyguards, was cut down while waiting at a Compton stoplight. In rapid succession, "Buntry" McDonald and "Hen Dog" Smith, both also closely allied with Suge, were summarily executed. In early 2000 "V" Buchanan, a Blood drug dealer, was found dead in a Compton graveyard from a single shot to the back of his head. Next up was another of Suge's closest confidants, Wardell "Poochie" Fouse. Poochie had barely sur-vived an attack in April 2000 when he was ambushed and severely wounded. Three years later he was shot ten times in the back as he rode a motorcycle across a Compton intersection. The killing had been preceded a few months earlier by a late-night attack on the Death Row offices, shattering windows and blowing holes in the stucco of the Wilshire Boulevard building.

"If somebody's planning to hunt me down," Suge scornfully remarked in a 2003 *L.A. Times* article, "they are going to have to be more serious about their business. They drive by my building…and shoot the front windows out. Look out, they killed my windows! Who do they think they're kidding?"

The Internal Revenue Service, for one, was not kidding. In 2006 it hit Suge with a $6 million bill for back taxes. Shortly afterward, he filed for bankruptcy. The mortgage holder of the bullet-riddled Death Row headquarters threatened seizure of the office furniture; his skybox at the Staples Center was revoked for missed payments, and his ninety-foot yacht was repossessed. Questioned by creditors, he denied rumors of having a large stash of cash and precious metals hidden away in an overseas bank. He listed among his remaining assets a thousand dollars in clothing, two thousand dollars in furnishings, and eleven dollars in a bank account. The only item of any worth was some jewelry that he valued at $25,000. Whether that included one of the coveted Death Row medallions is unknown.

The downward spiral continued in the wake of Suge's financial meltdown. In the summer of 2005 he was caught in the crossfire of a shootout at a party hosted by the rapper Kanye West. Wounded in the upper leg, he later sued West for pain, suffering, and the theft of a fifteen-carat diamond earring. A few months later he was badly beaten in Scottsdale, Arizona, by the business manager of the rapper Akon. While the reason for the assault was never made clear, the outcome was as plain as the broken nose and shattered bones in Suge's face. A few months later he was implicated in the robbery of Akon's producer Noel "Detail" Fisher, in which $170,000 worth of bling was stolen. No charges were ever pressed in that case, nor in a 2008 incident when he was arrested for aggravated assault in Las Vegas after police arrived outside a strip club to find him beating his girlfriend senseless. Suffice it to say, by the time we began focusing our investigation on Suge, he was a shadow of his former self, running small-time hustles out of a tract home in Las Vegas.

As it turned out, the trail we were following had been well traveled before us. In another side benefit of the case being federalized, we were given access to the voluminous files of an extensive joint operation between the FBI and the ATF, looking into racketeering activities at Death Row and its role as an arm of the Mob Piru's ongoing criminal conspiracy.

The agencies' investigation had gotten up and running in 1994 and was given added impetus a year later when Suge and his Death Row posse were involved in a pair of brutal incidents. The first was the murder of a Rolling '60s Crip stomped to death at the El Rey Theater, where a Death Row party was being held. A participant in the event told the FBI in 1996 that a verbal altercation broke out between the victim and several Death Row associates, leading to the savage assault. According to the witness, Suge had stood on the sidelines, urging on his enforcers with a shout of "Ya'll get that nigger."

The second incident was the assault and torture of a New York record promoter named Mark Anthony Bell. According to a statement Bell made to the LAPD in 1995, Suge had invited him to a Christmas party at a rented home in the Hollywood Hills. It was there that Bell was taken to an upstairs room where Suge and some associates tried to force him to reveal the whereabouts of Puffy. Knight, Bell speculated, held Combs responsible for the Atlanta nightclub shooting of Jake Robles earlier that year and was looking for payback. When Bell refused to cooperate, Suge ordered his cohorts to beat him, cautioning them to use "body blows only." According to Bell's account, one of the assailants told him, "I could kill you right now if Suge says so." He subsequently attempted to jump off the balcony after Knight returned from the bathroom with a champagne glass full of urine and tried to make him drink it.

"I don't piss in champagne glasses," Suge later remarked. It was as close as he would come to claiming his innocence in the attack.

The incidents were added to a growing list of potential prosecutions stemming from the federal investigation. But the FBI and the ATF had bigger fish to fry, as their case reached beyond racketeering allegations and back down the well-worn track of possible LAPD involvement. The old charge of rogue officers on the Death Row payroll would become an important aspect of the federal probe, as did the connection between Suge and Deputy District Attorney Larry Longo of L.A. County. It was Longo who had recommended a nine-year "suspended" sentence for Suge after his conviction for pistol-whipping the aspiring rap producer Lynwood Stanley and his brother George. To federal investigators the sentence seemed suspiciously lenient, especially considering that after serving a month in a halfway house, Suge moved into Longo's exclusive Malibu Colony beach home. At the same time, the deputy DA's daughter, Gina Longo, became the first white artist to be signed to Death Row Records, with a $50,000 advance. Although Longo had been fired as a result of his cozy connection with Suge, the federal task force had good reason to wonder how much further Knight's influence might have extended into City Hall.

In the end, however, the FBI and ATF investigation ran up hard against the effects of September 11, and the massive reallocation of manpower at the federal level that followed. Directives changed overnight, with the emphasis on homeland security trumping everything. After seven long years, attempts by federal authorities to make a RICO case against Suge Knight had reached an impasse. Yet there was no denying that what had been accomplished was impressive. The agencies, cultivating a wide range of informants, had put together the first coherent picture of how gangs had infiltrated the music industry and used the record business as a front for drug dealing, money laundering, and tax evasion. There's no question that the foundations of a racketeering case had been laid. But without funding and manpower, it all added up to little more then the mound of files that our task force had inherited. It would be up to us to take the next step.

Suge Knight (center) and his Mob Piru posse, all of whom are deceased except George Williams (standing far right) who is serving a a 25-year prison term.

CHAPTER 19

The Impala

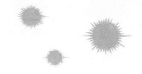

A S ABUNDANT AS THE record against Suge Knight might have been, there was a specific category of crimes that we became interested in after taking a look at the seven-year federal investigation. It was immediately clear, from the work they had done, that racketeering was the most promising avenue to pursue.

There was little doubt that Sugar Bear was a dangerous individual. But what would make a difference in court would be our ability to establish not simply his personal history of mayhem, but rather his corporate criminal activities. Any RICO case depends entirely on proving an ongoing pattern of criminal activities. Murder, assault, robbery, extortion, fraud; any one of those charges could carry significant penalties when tried as separate counts. But such penalties expanded exponentially if they could be shown to be part of a continuing criminal venture. If we could prove that Death Row Records, for example, was funded, in whole or in part, by the sale of narcotics, we would have a viable RICO case and could put Suge away for a long time.

To that end, Daryn and I put a premium on reviving a relationship the federal task force had made with Michael "Harry O" Harris. One of the most successful crack dealers in the country, Harry O had used his ill-gotten gains to fund a range of successful legitimate businesses. Before age thirty he owned and operated a fleet of limousines, a Beverly Hills hair salon, a high-end auto dealership, a construction company, and a delicatessen. He also had his hand in a number of show business ventures, funding Rap-a-Lot Records, a Houston hip-hop label that was home to the hit Geto Boys, and producing two hit Broadway plays, one of which starred Denzel Washington at just the point when the young actor's career was starting to take off.

In 1987, his empire came crashing down when he was convicted on attempted murder and drug charges and was sent to San Quentin to serve a twenty-eight-year sentence. But even behind bars, Harry O's entrepreneurial flair was in evidence. He became editor of the *San Quentin News*, wrote a book of short stories on prison life, and, more to the point, continued to expand his investment portfolio, using drug funds he had hidden from government seizure. According to interviews he had given to the FBI during their Death Row investigation, Harry O had had more than twenty cell block visits from Suge Knight, and as a result of these discussions agreed to put $1.5 million into Knight's proposed new rap start-up, Death Row Records. Shortly thereafter, Death Row's megahit *The Chronic* was released and Suge signed a lucrative distribution deal with Interscope Records, cutting his incarcerated investor out of the profits in the process. "I was betrayed," Harris claimed in an interview with the *Los Angeles Times*. "Michael Harris makes things up to try and get out of jail," was Suge's reply and it certainly came as no surprise that he would indignantly deny a partnership with the jailed drug dealer. If it could be proven that Death Row was launched with drug money, the linchpin of a criminal conspiracy case would be in place

It was with that in mind that Daryn and I paid a call on Harry O. Our hope was that we could pick up where the FBI had left off and try to nail down his claim that he had helped to finance Death Row with crack cocaine money. At six feet five, Harris was an imposing presence; pound for pound every bit the equal of Suge. He listened impassively as we made our case by suggesting that, in exchange for some hard facts on his investment deal, maybe we could be of assistance in his ongoing efforts to get out of prison.

But Harry O had something else in mind. He wanted us to investigate the 1998 drowning death of his brother, which he had good reason to believe was not an accident: David Harris was himself active in the drug trade and had been the target of two separate homicide investigations. Yet, as Daryn and I took a closer look at the death, it became clear that there had been no foul play. Not that we could convince Harry O of the fact. When we returned to San Quentin with the news, he dismissed us with a wave of his huge hand and walked out of the meeting. Our hope of eliciting his testimony to establish a RICO case against Suge had run aground. The enterprising inmate meanwhile returned to his primary activity: mounting a $107 million lawsuit against Suge Knight over Harris's original Death Row investment. An eventual decision in his favor was, along with the $6 million IRS claim, a precipitating factor in Suge's bankruptcy declaration.

As it would turn out, Suge's bankruptcy provided us with another opportunity to build a plausible RICO case. As part of the disposal of his assets and distribution of the proceeds, the bankruptcy trustee examined what else might be in his possession aside from the eleven dollars that he claimed comprised his liquid assets. As a result, more than ten thousand Death Row recordings were inventoried and their value assessed.

It was shortly afterward that we were contacted by detectives from the Livingston County Sheriff's Department in western Michigan, giving us a heads-up on an intriguing case that had developed in their jurisdiction. Carl "Butch" Smalls was a former Suge Knight associate who had worked at Death Row and nurtured musical ambitions of his own. His dreams of stardom eventually dashed, Smalls moved to Michigan where he lived with his girlfriend. Their often violent relationship culminated in an assault that prompted the battered girlfriend to move out. Gathering her belongings, she went to a storage facility the two had rented when they had first consolidated households. It was there that she discovered recording-studio hard drives and master tapes, their labels designating them as property of Death Row Records. Confronting Butch, she was told that he had been ordered by Suge Knight to hide the cache of music when Death Row was going under. She reported her discovery to the local authorities and, more to the point, to the bankruptcy court that was handling Suge's Chapter 11 proceedings. Not long after, we were made aware of the find.

The link to our investigation was obvious. Suge had sworn in bankruptcy court that Death Row's assets had been duly disclosed. Yet here was a substantial hoard of recordings that not only had not been declared, but had been deliberately concealed from authorities. Jeff Bennett and I flew to Detroit, immediately seized the contents of the storage space, and had them shipped back to Los Angeles for examination. Scrutinized by the bankruptcy trustees, it was determined that the tapes and digital masters contained more than a thousand previously unreleased songs from some of Death Row's top artists, including a half dozen unheard Tupac Shakur originals. The estimated value of the music: $20 million. Apprised of our find, Assistant U.S. Attorney Tim Searight immediately added bankruptcy fraud to the growing catalog of Suge Knight's possible RICO violations.

Bankruptcy; the wholesale death or defection of his artists; the total collapse of his record label: none of it seemed to convince Suge that he wasn't still a major music-business player, whether anyone else thought so. In early 2008, Suge accordingly arrived at the front gate of the famed producer and executive Jimmy Iovine's estate. Chauffeuring him for the occasion was an Eight-Seven Crip who at the time was also an at-large parolee considered armed and dangerous. Summoning the security guard through an intercom, Suge announced that he had come to party with his old friend Jimmy.

Iovine had, in fact, once been tight with Suge, back when Knight had first signed the distribution deal with Interscope Records, at a time when they both needed a change of fortune. The Brooklyn-born Iovine had begun his career as a recording engineer, working with the likes of John Lennon and Bruce Springsteen before becoming one of the hottest producers of the eighties. In 1990 he formed the independent Interscope Records, but the start-up sputtered and was about to go under when Iovine induced Suge to bring Death Row Records under his label's umbrella. It was a canny move, considering the impending gangsta rap phenomenon, which Iovine did much to promote and popularize. Success bonded the ambitious pair until Suge's increasingly erratic behavior became too much for Iovine to tolerate. In 1997, the two parted ways, but not before Iovine poached some of Suge's biggest-selling artists, including Snoop Dogg. In early 2008, Snoop released *Ego Trippin'* on Interscope. It was in celebration of the album's first single that Iovine had thrown a party that night.

There was only one problem: the event wasn't being held at Iovine's home. In fact, Iovine wasn't on the premises, having earlier left for the party. Informed of that fact by security personnel, Suge and his escort proceeded to cruise the perimeter of the property, all the while being watched on closed-circuit cameras from inside the guard shack. When they pulled up next to the service entrance, a pack of German shepherds was released, chasing the intruders away. The next morning, a disturbed Jimmy Iovine contacted Chief William Bratton directly. Daryn and I, along with Bill Holcomb, were dispatched to interview the record executive, and it was clear from the beginning that he had been rattled by Knight's sudden appearance. He hadn't had contact with Suge for years, Iovine explained, and considered his sudden appearance as a thinly veiled threat, either in retaliation for the Snoop Dogg signing or to extort money from his old business associate. He wanted it dealt with right away, but for the moment all we could do was file away the complaint in Suge's growing dossier of potentially indictable crimes.

But we wouldn't get a real break in our efforts to put Suge behind bars until we focused our attention on a possible extortion and fraud case. It was, at that time, the first new incident of Knight's criminal activity that we had uncovered on our own, which meant that witness recollection would be a lot fresher than some of the decade-old allegations we were trying to resurrect.

Among the many uncanny aspects of the Tupac and Biggie murder investigations, was the way in which certain clues kept reappearing and repeating, mirroring the same startling similarities. So it was with a vintage Chevrolet Impala. The make of vehicle had first appeared as the drive-by car outside the Petersen. Now, another Impala was about to become one of our most important pieces of evidence against Suge Knight.

In 1996, Knight had hired an auto restorer named Juventino Yanez. According to a 1999 DEA report, Yanez was a "well known cocaine distributor, believed to be distributing as many as fifty kilograms of cocaine per week," out of his auto shop. But Suge's deal with Juventino actually involved legitimate restoration. For a cool $30,000, he was hired to bring a vintage 1961 Impala back to its pristine showroom condition. The car was to be presented to Tupac with an airbrushed rendering of the cover art for his forthcoming *All Eyez on Me* album splashed across the deck. But Tupac never had a chance to enjoy the lavish gift. Just prior to its completion, he was gunned down in Las Vegas.

After the murder of its intended owner, the Impala passed through many owners, beginning with Tupac's mother, Afeni, who was reputedly given the car by Suge in memory of her son. But it was Yanez who retained the vehicle's pink slip, even after he lost possession of the car itself. The Impala, in fact, traded hands a number of times before ending up in the possession of Armando Hermosillo, owner of an El Monte body shop. Hermosillo had bought the car, without the pink slip, for $15,000, and after obtaining a duplicate title he proudly put it on display in the street outside his business to attract customers. It was there, in the late summer of 2006, that the Impala was spotted by Yanez's son, who returned the next day with his father. "I built that car for Suge Knight," Yanez told the body shop owner, insisting that the Impala was rightfully his because, as he put it, "I pulled a lot of time for those guys." The time to which he referred was a prison sentence Yanez served after police discovered a cache of guns hidden in his garage.

Hermosillo was not impressed and Yanez left without the Impala. A few weeks later Yanez's son returned to the body shop, this time in the company of a contingent of Bloods. Once again Armando held his ground, until he was handed a cell phone. On the other end: Suge Knight. "That car belongs to the industry," Suge informed the body shop owner. "Give it over. I have my own cops. I'll call them. You know what I can do to you." Hermosillo stepped aside as the vehicle was loaded on a flatbed tow truck and driven away.

But the saga of the '61 Impala with the Tupac paint job didn't end there. A few weeks later a friend and fellow officer who worked for the Bell Gardens Police Department, and happened to be the brother-in-law of Armando Hermosillo, contacted me. It was clear from what he told me that we had the makings of a possible extortion case, based on Suge's none-too-subtle threat to call out his own enforcers if Hermosillo didn't cooperate. The Impala had provided us with a very lucky break, if we could back up Hermosillo's account

The 1961 Impala with the custom paint job that Suge Knight had planned on presenting to Tupac Shakur shortly before the rapper's murder.

of the fear and intimidation Suge had employed to gain possession of the car.

As it turned out, Suge hadn't held on to the prized vehicle for very long. When we were finally able to track it down, we found it in hock in the back lot of a Long Beach pawnshop. Considering that by some estimates the ride was worth upward of $75,000, the pawnbrokers had gotten a deal. With the Impala as collateral, they had made a loan for a mere $20,000. We promptly impounded the car and brought it back to Armando Hermosillo. Our plan was to use it as bait to draw out more extortion threats from Suge. Anticipating that eventuality, we installed cameras in Hermosillo's shop and sat back to wait for our trap to be sprung.

Before that could happen, however, the case would take yet another strange and unpredictable twist.

CHAPTER 20

Stutterbox

J UST AS THE SEPARATE GEARS of the investigation that we
had set in motion began to mesh, we got a call from an FBI agent
who was working with an informant he thought might prove useful to us. His name was Robert Ross. The agent had been actively
investigating Ross' gang, the Main Street Crips, and, he informed
us, Ross had been helpful in providing inside information.

Ross went by the name "Stutterbox,"—"Box" for short—a reference to his habit of stammering when he got excited or scared. We
made arrangements to meet the informant at a Westside Starbucks,
and as we pulled into the parking lot on that crisp November morning,
we spotted a man sitting in the driver's seat of a white Rolls-Royce
Phantom.

Daryn and I looked at each other. Could this flamboyant individual be the guy we had come to talk to? But by that time Stutterbox,
flashing a large diamond stud earring, had gotten out of the Rolls

and was walking toward us. Even if we didn't immediately recognize him, he seemed to know cops when he saw them.

And that wasn't all that he knew. Much like Keffe D's claim, Stutterbox seemed confident that what he had to tell us would blow our minds. And, in fact, his information *did* at first seem to be a game changer. Suge Knight, he revealed, was involved in a multi-kilo cocaine trafficking operation using a Mexican supplier. If we wanted proof, all we needed to do was set up surveillance on a truck driver named Cash Jones.

A onetime Pacoima Piru, Stutterbox continued, Cash Jones was Suge's primary courier, running dope on a route up and down the West Coast from Washington State to National City, just below San

(Left to right) Robert "Stutterbox" Ross, Suge Knight and Cash Jones.
Stutterbox would later be implicated in an alleged extortion attempt
against basketball great Shaquille O'Neal.

Diego near the Mexican border. Jones, an operator-owner at a trucking firm, had a rig specially built to transport high-end autos—an echo of Kevin Davis's operation to run dope from California to Virginia using his auto-restoration business. When we asked Ross how he was privy to this information, he told us that he and Jones were old friends. The two, in fact, had met with Suge in Las Vegas in the company of the alleged Mexican dealer.

It was, on the face of it, a credible story and became more so when Daryn and I checked out as many of the details of Stutterbox's account as we could. Although Cash Jones had a relatively slim rap sheet—a few juvenile offences were all we could find—he had indeed been associated with the Pacoima Piru. But, more than any single corroborating detail, the overriding fact was that Stutterbox was an FBI source. If he was good enough for them, we had more than enough reason to give him the benefit of the doubt.

Accordingly, we put a GPS device on Jones's truck, enabling us to track where he was and where he was going at any given time. But he discovered the unit after an impromptu brake inspection at a highway rest stop. Alarmed at the strange black box stuck up under his chassis, he threw it into a field and notified the local police that someone had planted a bomb on his rig. Since we also had a wiretap on his cell phone, we were able to intercept the call, quickly contact the local authorities, and on the spot come up with a quasi-plausible story for them to tell the distraught Jones: a ring of sophisticated car thieves were using trackers to steal vehicles off the back of transport trucks. It was pretty lame, but Jones bought it, probably because there was no other credible explanation being offered.

The fact was, the closer we looked at Cash Jones, the more it became apparent that he was supporting his comfortable lifestyle by simple hard work. When he wasn't on long-haul trips, he was running a number of small but completely legitimate sidelines, including distributing a men's magazine called *Straight Stuntin'*. It might have been sleazy, but it wasn't illegal, and as time went on we gained increasing respect for the truck driver's entrepreneurial spirit.

At the same time, Stutterbox's credibility took a sharp dive. Regardless of his FBI connection, his information was proving to be less than reliable. Far from running drugs for Suge Knight, Cash Jones was the picture of legitimate enterprise. Did our informant have some ulterior motive in cooperating with us? We decided it was time to take a closer look into Box.

What we found rocked our world—again. As we were making a routine review of some of the early Biggie Smalls case files, we found the nickname "Stutterbox" linked to the clues provided to Russell Poole by the jailhouse informant Michael Robinson. Robinson had claimed he had solid information that Biggie's killer was a member of the paramilitary Fruit of Islam and a close associate of a Crip known as Stutterbox. But that was just the beginning. Running a documents check, Daryn discovered that in 1995 Robert Ross had applied for a California driver's license under another name: Amir Muhammad.

I remember staring in disbelief at the report Dupree handed me. A dozen different thoughts were chasing around my head. Amir Muhammad was, of course, the alias name of Harry Billups, college roommate of corrupt Rampart cop David Mack and the man who, Russell Poole was convinced, had killed Biggie Smalls. The theory had been discredited, or so we thought. Now, suddenly, Amir Muhammad was back, this time in the guise of Stutterbox.

Pouring over the transcript of Michael Robinson's jailhouse interview, I felt a growing sense of incredulity and the stomach-churning sensation that whatever was going on went deeper than we could ever have imagined. Robinson had insisted that the shooter at the Petersen was a Black Muslim. Stutterbox had made the claim to us that he was a nephew of the Nation of Islam leader, Louis Farrakhan. Was Robert Ross Amir Muhammad? Was he an associate of Amir

Muhammad's? And whoever he was, or said he was, why had he suddenly turned up on our doorstep, offering to help with information on a Suge Knight drug ring? Was Stutterbox playing us, trying to get inside the investigation to find out exactly what we knew about who had killed Biggie Smalls and why? And if so, was he trying to throw us completely off the trail in the process?

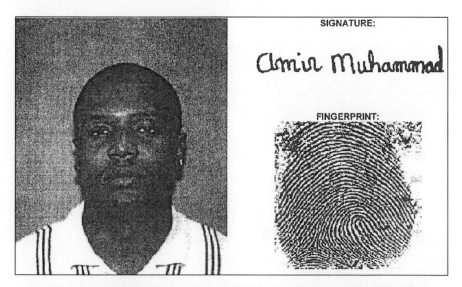

SIGNATURE:

Amir Muhammad

FINGERPRINT:

The driver's license photo of Robert "Stutterbox' Ross, as Amir Muhammad. His dual identity would, for a time, lead investigators to believe Biggie Smalls' killer may have infiltrated the investigation.

It was beginning to look like any of those scenarios, singly or in combination, might be true. In the weeks that followed, as we struggled to make sense of the strange new dimensions the case had taken, the investigation seemed at times to be collapsing in on itself, the same information repeating in different situations and circumstances until it became impossible to know what was real and what was a fantasy formulated by Stutterbox.

The situation reached an extreme when I flew to Atlanta to talk to another informant who claimed to have information on the Main Street Crips. I almost had to laugh when he told me that Stutterbox had been a hit man for Eric "Zip" Martin. The sense of unreality was subsequently ratcheted up when Stutterbox himself came to us with a another news flash: he had it on good authority that Duane "Keffe D" Davis was personally planning to rob one of the principals in the George Torres case I had investigated nearly ten years earlier.

While it was impossible to attribute all these converging signs to mere coincidence, it was equally out of the question that all this would somehow, some way, fit together into a coherent whole. It was just too hard to believe that this entire cast of characters was so completely interconnected in a case that now seemed to have no boundaries or borders, no beginning or end. Our investigation was threatening to come apart at the seams.

But it would only get stranger as Stutterbox increasingly became an enigmatic and sinister presence that, at times, seemed to be laughing at us. Yet regardless of the doubts that surrounded him was the simple fact that he fit some of the criteria for the shooter at the Petersen. Not least among them was his Amir Muhammad moniker and Nation of Islam connections. When we questioned him about the name, he insisted that he had started using it only in 1998, after being converted to the faith in prison. But we had evidence that proved otherwise, in the form of his 1995 driver's license made out to Amir Muhammad. Why was he trying to hide the fact that he had been known by that name for more than two years prior to the murder of Biggie Smalls?

As it turned out, Ross was harboring even more secrets and lies. Shortly after we started looking into his past and present activities, it was revealed that he was a prime suspect in a Los Angeles Sheriff's Department fraud investigation, involving a crew of several women who cashed bogus checks at local banks. The operation, over which Stutterbox allegedly presided, had netted upward of $11 million at the time of the investigation. As part of its probe, the Sheriff's Department had obtained the cell phone of one of Stutterbox's female accomplices. Downloading the photos stored on it, they found—along with a number of nude poses by the woman—a photo of Stutterbox, decked out in even more expensive jewelry and brandishing a handgun with typical gangbanger bravado. Further examination of the weapon revealed it to be a .9 mm, the same type of gun that had taken out Biggie. That wasn't all. The way Ross was holding the gun, using both hands to brace it and holding it at eye level for maximum accuracy, suggested to us that he was familiar with the use of firearms. Was this yet another indicator that Stutterbox was, in fact, the shooter?

Before we could find the answer, Ross upped the ante when he became the unlikely victim of a kidnapping and robbery, an incredible plot twist in an already improbable story. According to his account, he had been abducted from his Rolls while on the streets of West Hollywood by members of his own gang, the Main Street Crips, supposedly acting on orders of their much-feared leader, Ladell "Del Dog" Rowles. Pistol-whipped and robbed of his bling, he was forced to drive to a South Central neighborhood deep in the gang's territory, where he was released on the promise that he immediately return with $60,000 in cash.

Instead, he placed a frantic call to Daryn, begging for help. Dupree instructed him to contact the nearest law enforcement authorities. Sheriff's officers were duly summoned and the story Stutterbox related to them managed to trump even the wildest tale he had told us. According to his account, he had been kidnapped by the Main Street Crips in retaliation for an elaborate blackmail scheme he had hatched to incriminate none other than the basketball legend Shaquille O'Neal.

Stutterbox claimed to have once been Shaq's unofficial social director, organizing parties and functions for the sports star in and around the Los Angeles area. At one such event, Stutterbox would also assert, Shaq had ostensibly been filmed having sex with a woman other than his wife and Box had allegedly attempted to extort money by threatening to make the sex tapes public.

But the fantastic story didn't stop there. O'Neal, as part of his role-model responsibilities, had agreed to participate in a South Central L.A. community outreach, lending his name to a campaign to raise money for children's holiday gifts. The organizer of the event was none other than "Del Dog" Rowles, in a public-image ploy that is hardly unusual among gangsters. It was Stutterbox's contention that Del Dog had taken exception to the extortion plot he had hatched against Shaq, and that the kidnapping and manhandling had been a warning for him to cease and desist.

It seemed more likely to us that he was actually being punished for not kicking back enough to the gang from his bank fraud operation, especially considering that Del Dog was known for requiring regular contributions from every Main Street Crip. But Sheriff's Department investigators had a whole different take, immediately seeing the potential for a high-profile, headline-grabbing case. For sheriff's investigators, Stutterbox was the victim of a criminal conspiracy. To us, he was the potential killer of Biggie Smalls. The whole notion that Shaq had been involved in such a caper was absurd on its face, yet another manifestation of Stutterbox's runaway imagination.

But perhaps there was more to it. Maybe Box's intention all along was to set the LAPD and the Sheriff's Department at odds. Tension developed over how to handle the case, even reaching into the task force itself, where team members on loan from the sheriff made it known that they disapproved of our efforts to establish a link between Ross and the murder we were investigating.

While it produced no sign of a sex tape, a subsequent search of Stutterbox's home did turn up a good deal of O'Neal memorabilia, including a large autographed shoe, an NBA championship ring, and various photos of Shaq in the company of a beaming Stutterbox. The mementoes certainly strengthened his story of a connection between the two, but by that time I wasn't buying anything he had to say, not without proof that I could touch, taste, and, if necessary, smell. I'd gone about as far down the yellow brick road with him as I cared to go.

Box's whole house of cards finally collapsed when two South Central patrol officers received a call regarding a Lexus IS with no license plates being driven erratically down Martin Luther King Jr. Boulevard, nearly striking a stoplight and straddling two lanes. The vehicle was pursued until it swung wide down a side street and abruptly came to a stop. Approaching the car, the officers detected pot smoke and saw the driver frantically attempting to conceal what later turned out to be a cache of rock cocaine and Ecstasy in the form of blue pills stamped with the image of a smiling Buddha.

It was Stutterbox. Skittish and high as a kite, he fled again as the officers approached the Lexus, and another high-speed chase ensued until he collided with a parked car and attempted to carjack a passing vehicle. Officers arrived as the frightened driver took off, leaving Ross to stumble down the street until he was apprehended and arrested. In a subsequent search of the area, officers discovered a stolen handgun Stutterbox had thrown away during the chase.

Suddenly, the tables were turned. With his prior history of narcotics and weapons convictions, we'd be able to hold hefty federal charges over his head, compelling his cooperation instead of the other way around. The Sheriff's Department still insisted they wanted him as a material witness in the kidnapping case, but the U.S. attorney took our side and agreed to prosecute him on multiple counts. We had finally gotten Stutterbox in a box.

At that point, I was just relieved at the prospect of putting him behind bars until we could figure out exactly what part he played in all the interlocking aspects of the case. Dealing with Stutterbox had been exhausting, not least because of his ability to throw us off the track by opening up new possibilities just when we needed to narrow our options. Which is not to say we still weren't haunted by the way he had found his way into our investigation. But sometimes coincidences are just that: accidents of fact and circumstance without any larger significance except maybe the haphazard workings of the universe. Sometimes Amir Muhammad is just a name. Sometimes the way a gangster holds a gun just means he's watched one too many cop shows. In the end, the strange saga of Stutterbox added up to no more than a string of random occurrences expertly orchestrated by a masterful con artist.

Still, we had to follow it through to the end. After his arrest, we gave Stutterbox a lie detector test, asking him specifically about his knowledge of the Biggie Smalls murder. I'm not a big believer in polygraphs, especially when it comes to a subject like Stutterbox. His whole life, in one way or another, had been a lie. Did he even know what the truth *was* anymore? I had my doubts that lines on graph paper would serve to clear up the mystery of his complicity. Predictably, the results left us with more questions than answers. Stutterbox, the polygraph examiner informed us, had failed the test miserably. But what did that even mean? It might have confirmed that he knew nothing about the Biggie killing and was making up a story as he went along. Or it might be that he really *did* know who had done the deed and couldn't pretend that he didn't.

Either way it didn't much matter. After months of bewildering complications, we had finally cleared away the smoke and mirrors surrounding Stutterbox. At that point my concern was that he'd never again have an opportunity to interfere with an investigation. I made it my business to draft a letter deeming him to be what is technically termed an Unreliable Informant. I couldn't have thought of a better description if I'd tried.

PART
SIX

CHAPTER 21

Theresa

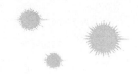

B Y THE SPRING OF 2009, the task force had been at work on the Biggie Smalls murder investigation and its ties to the death of Tupac Shakur for almost two years. In one respect we had made a lot of progress. Keffe D had led us to believe that it was Baby Lane Anderson who pulled the trigger in Las Vegas. If we could elicit confirmation of his account from Zip, half our case could well be made.

Which left the other half, and in that regard we had reached a frustrating impasse. As preparations proceeded to send Keffe D back to New York for a rendezvous with Zip, we took a hard look at the options left to us for breaking the Biggie case itself.

There weren't many. Absent some major new revelation, we had pretty much exhausted every possibility that might lead to identifying the killer or killers. We had managed to eliminate many of the persistent rumors and half-truths that had for so long obscured the facts, but we weren't any closer to uncovering precisely what those facts might actually be. Our surreal interlude with Stutterbox had proved how easy it was to get lost in the twists and turns of the investigation. After years of dogged effort, a definitive answer as to who killed Biggie and why had become an ever more elusive goal.

But we kept at it. We were convinced that somewhere in those file cabinets of police reports, interview transcripts, documents, and photographs comprising the sum total of the case, *something* had been overlooked. Because of our success in gaining Keffe D's cooperation, we put our efforts into finding another candidate we could utilize in the same way. The problem wasn't that there weren't enough possible contenders. Almost every key individual with a role in the case had a checkered past and an uncertain future. What was needed was someone in Suge Knight's inner circle privy to his most closely guarded secrets. It was there, we felt sure, that we would find the key to unlock the truth behind Biggie's murder.

So we went back to square one, taking yet another pass at the federal probe into Death Row's racketeering activities beginning in 1995, sifting through the welter of investigative details for something, anything, that might have escaped our attention. As the painstaking search went on, we gradually began to focus on a forty-two-year-old single mother of two by the name of Theresa Swann.

At first we weren't really sure exactly whom we were dealing with. Swann seemed to have a number of distinct personas, revealed on a series of California driver's license photos taken under ten different aliases in as many years. On one, her attractive features cluster around large dark eyes, radiating a look of wary regard for the world and its mess of troubles. On another, a middle-aged black woman with hoop earrings and straight, shoulder-length hair smiles into the camera. In yet another, a decidedly foxy party girl, heavily made up and strikingly attractive, fixes the camera with a cool appraising look. On a license issued in 2000, Theresa sports a modified afro that now lent her a slightly militant air. Two years earlier, she came off as a flirtatious forties vamp in a processed flip, her lips dark red. She had almost as many names as faces: Theresa Rennell Swann, Theresa Jazzmin Swann, Tamee Swann, Theresa Reed, Teresa Lynn Cross, and other variations on the theme. But as we closely studied all those pictures, tracking all the changes she had put herself through, it was hard to get a fix on who the real Theresa Swann might be. And the harder we looked, the more we wanted to know.

But the details of her life were likewise sketchy and contradictory. Born in Ohio, Theresa was one of three children sired by a pimp and small-time hustler. After the family fell apart, her mother took Theresa, her sister, and her brother west to Long Beach. Several years later Theresa, by now a strikingly attractive young woman, caught Suge's eye. But she wasn't the only one. Aside from his long-suffering wife, Sharitha, Suge's roster of steady girlfriends—as distinguished from occasional hookups—included Michelle Toussaint, a vocalist known as Michel'le he had signed to Death Row. In this crowded field Theresa initially stood out. Aside from her good looks, she had curried Suge's favor by becoming his all-purpose go-to girl, ready and willing to roll with him on any number of criminal enterprises. Before long she had transformed herself, for all intents and purposes, into his accomplice. She also joined the burgeoning ranks of Suge's baby mamas, giving birth to Suge's daughter in 2004.

Nevertheless, Theresa found herself constantly competing for Suge's attention with Sharitha and Michel'le, both of whom had prior claims and their own offspring to back them up. Michel'le, in particular, gave Theresa a run for her money. She was far and away Suge's favorite, with his attraction measured in, among other things, cold cash. After he was sent back to prison on the MGM Grand parole violation Suge arranged for his brother-in-law Norris Anderson to keep his business and personal affairs in order. The day-to-day administration of Death Row became Norris's responsibility, as did the doling out of support payments to Suge's women. Both Theresa and Sharitha received a paltry $1,500 a month from the father of their children. Michel'le's stipend, on the other hand, was a hefty $10,000.

Suge even went so far as to devise an elaborate scheme to allow Michel'le conjugal visits while he was serving his sentence. This prison privilege, of course, is extended only to husband and wife, and Suge had no intention of dumping the dependable Sharitha. Instead, he induced his brother-in-law Norris Anderson to pose as Suge Knight at the altar, marry Michel'le and thus clear the way for her to satisfy his needs behind bars on a regular basis. For his part Anderson denies any involvement in the charade, and handwriting analysis of the marriage certificate proved inconclusive. It is, nevertheless, interesting to speculate that Michel'le might have became the second wife of Norris Anderson, or maybe Suge Knight, or maybe both of them, depending on how you looked at it.

Whatever she may have lacked in competition with her younger rival, Theresa tried to make up for in sheer unstinting devotion to Suge. In the nearly two decades of their relationship, she carried out a remarkable range of illegal activities on his behalf, from fraud to fencing to tax evasion and beyond, in the process becoming his de facto white-collar-criminal proxy. But that wasn't her only role. On occasion Theresa was a source of almost maternal comfort, as demonstrated when Suge was involved in one of his periodic brawls, this one leaving him bleeding and battered on a Hollywood street before being hauled away by his posse. He was taken directly to Theresa, who treated his wounds with tender, loving care.

But it was her function as his criminal consort that most interested us. Not that Theresa didn't possess her own well-honed criminal tendencies: She was arrested in 1991 on Grand Theft Property charges and a year later served a brief jail sentence for possession of a controlled substance. But by 1993 she was firmly under Suge's sway, doing his exclusive bidding, and it was through meticulously reconstructing the record of their relationship that we came to realize how essential

Theresa Swann was to Suge Knight and his ambitions. Her name appeared early in the federal Death Row investigation as the "straw purchaser" of a Ferrari Testarossa, bought outright for $75,000 in cash. Registered to her, it was almost certainly Suge's ride. Shortly thereafter, she was listed as the president, secretary, and treasurer of Simon Productions, a Nevada company that served as a front for Death Row. There seemed to us an obvious link between the two businesses: Suge had had the nickname "Simon" since childhood, as in the game Simon Says: when Simon said it, you did it.

It was through Simon Productions that an operating license had been obtained for Suge's Las Vegas nightspot, Club 662, a transaction rumored to involve a payoff to a senior investigator for the Clark County Department of Business License. According to FBI reports, Swann was instrumental in finding a dummy owner and manager for the club, coaching the club's security guard on how to apply for the license and appear credible before the board. The guard was officially the manager when Club 662 opened in the late summer of 1996, operating it for only a few weekends prior to the fateful night of Tupac's death, after which it was closed for good.

In another intriguing wrinkle, Swann's name appeared on a transfer of ownership for a Los Angeles body shop that served as a Suge Knight front and was eventually sold to help fund Club 662. Theresa had, in fact, increasingly become the possessor of record on a number of assets that, in reality, were owned, or least claimed, by Suge. When, for example, Suge and his Piru posse hauled away the airbrushed 1961 Impala from outside Armando Hermosillo's garage, it was Theresa who subsequently pawned the car, signing for the loan in her name.

In order to accommodate all the fraudulent transactions Suge required, it was necessary for Theresa to assemble her gallery of false identities. Once we established that she was using multiple driver's licenses, we did a complete workup of her DMV history, cross-referencing birth dates, residences, fingerprints, and handwriting. We came up with a comprehensive catalog of the many faces of Theresa Swann, but it was not quite enough on which to proceed. Obtaining a driver's license under an assumed name is a felony punishable by up to three years in prison, but the statute is very rarely enforced and we had to have something more than the possibility of a small fine or suspended sentence to compel Theresa's cooperation.

So we kept looking, setting up surveillance of her house, once owned by Suge, in the middle-class suburb of Rancho Cucamonga, east of Los Angeles. It was there that Theresa lived with her daughter by Suge, as well as her teenage son from an earlier relationship. Also occupying the house was Theresa's brother, who at the time was out of prison on parole. The children attended nearby public schools and Theresa worked hard to create the appearance of a brave single mother doing her best to bring her kids up right.

Appearances were deceiving. Keeping a close eye on the location, we gathered increasing evidence of Theresa's ongoing association with Suge. Along with a Range Rover they both routinely drove, two other cars were often parked in the driveway of the ranch-style residence. The first was a Ford F150 pickup, decked out in a pricey black-and-red-trimmed Harley-Davidson package. Suge had used the truck up until the time he had been evicted from his high-priced West L.A. condo and had since stored it at the Rancho Cucamonga premises. The other vehicle was a Maserati Gran Turismo that Suge had once used to make an ostentatious appearance at a Blood's gang funeral. We looked into the sports car's history and discovered that it was registered in the name of Rodrigo Lopez, who Stutterbox had claimed was the alleged Mexican drug supplier that he had met in Las Vegas in the company of Suge. We would eventually set up a traffic stop specifically to pull Theresa over as she drove the Maserati around town. We were trying to establish another link between her and Suge, but we were really just shooting in the dark. It's not against the law to associate with a bad man, or even to visit him in jail seventy-five times over a two-year period. We needed something considerably more incriminating if we were going to get Theresa Swann to talk.

It was in late February 2009 that we finally began to open up the lead we were seeking. As part of our investigation into Knight's possible bankruptcy fraud, we'd found documents indicating that Suge had tried to transfer some Death Row master tapes to Theresa's name, thereby taking them off his liquidation list and out from under the scrutiny of the court. Looking closer at the possibility that Theresa had been an accessory to the deception, we discovered that the woman who had initially found the tape cache in a Detroit storage facility had subsequently received a call from Swann, who, she claimed, had made a number of thinly veiled threats. Since this was in large part a tax matter, we recruited an Internal Revenue Service agent to help us sort out the complex financial aspects of the investigation.

In the meantime we got word of even more significant charges being developed against Swann by the L.A. County Sheriff's Department. Their investigation targeted a sophisticated ring of thieves who submitted false auto-loan applications to buy vehicles, which they then turned around and sold for bargain prices. According to the sheriff's Commercial Crimes Unit, Swann was front and center in the operation. Accordingly, a raid on her residence was conducted by sheriff's deputies, during which a weapon first reported stolen in Seattle was recovered. Her brother, a former convict, was forbidden by law to have a weapon in the house and could potentially be charged with a weapons violation.

We now had several promising approaches to encourage Theresa's cooperation. She was arrested by the Sheriff's Department and subsequently informed of the charges pending against her as a key player in the auto-loan scam and the potential bankruptcy fraud, as well as complicity in her brother's weapons violation. The deputies suggested that Swann might want to talk with us, assuring her that, depending on her decision, they would hold off on making formal charges on the auto-loan counts. Swann tentatively agreed to the meeting.

It seemed at last that we had some real pressure to apply. But it was based on the premise that there was something more important in Theresa's life than loyalty to Suge Knight. There was no way to be certain, but we had reason to hope that retaining custody of her children might outweigh her twenty-year run with Sugar Bear.

CHAPTER 22

Starbucks

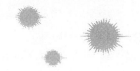

Even under duress, Theresa Swann still managed to put herself together nicely. She arrived at our meeting on March 17, 2009, stylishly attired in an outfit accentuating her slim, well-toned figure, sporting her trademark hoop earrings, her hair decorously pulled back and her makeup understated. She looked to all appearances like the upstanding suburban mom she had for so long pretended to be.

But it was clear from the deepening lines in her narrow face, and the way her eyes flickered with suspicion, that maintaining her double life was taking its toll. Gone was the sultry party girl who had gazed provocatively from the photos of her fake driver's license. The Theresa Swann who introduced herself to us that day in a low and uninflected voice had the kind of desperation that comes when every disguise is stripped away and there's no place left to hide.

We met her on a cloudless morning at a Starbucks in Santa Fe Springs. There's something about the soothing wood tones and the laid-back ambiance of a Starbucks that is conducive to this kind of charged encounter. It seems to put even the most wary criminal in a more amenable frame of mind, and that was an especially important consideration when it came to Theresa Swann.

To that end, Jeff Bennett had been in contact with her a few times prior to our sitdown. It wasn't that Daryn and I were going to play bad cop to Bennett's good cop. Rather, our aim was to provide a reference point for her, someone with whom she had become familiar, who had taken the time to listen to her story. Jeff got the job. It was a role we'd all played before, and while it might seem calculated it served an important purpose. We were about to ask Theresa Swann to do something that went against her every instinct: drop the dime on Suge Knight. To the degree that we were dealing with a woman who had made a career out of deception, we were sympathetic. But the reality was that she had brought this on herself. She had made the choice to become a willing accomplice to Suge Knight. What we hoped to do was to give her another option, to help her find a way out. It was a second chance that would begin with her coming clean.

Aside from Dupree, Bennett, and I, we had brought our IRS investigator along for the meeting. There was a good reason for such a conspicuous contingent. It was important for Theresa to assume that our questions would be confined to the matters at hand: the auto loan case being handled by sheriff's investigators and the bankruptcy fraud charges, which were under IRS jurisdiction. Depending on how *that* went, and as we evaluated her reaction to a charge of criminal complicity with Suge Knight, we could hopefully move on to topic A: the man himself.

If Swann was disconcerted to see four law enforcement officers waiting for her, she didn't show it. At least, there was no visible reaction in her expression as she sat down with her caramel macchiato. Instead, a steely skepticism hardened her features, belying any hint of fear or intimidation. Jeff Bennett's role notwithstanding, if we wanted to gain her trust we were going to have to earn it.

Initially she evinced no reaction when we outlined what she might be facing in the auto-loan case. It seemed likely that she was prepared to call our bluff on the charges and take her chances before a judge and jury. Then the IRS agent laid out the bankruptcy case with the kind of calm and professional dispassion that they must teach at IRS school. I watched Theresa's face carefully as he recited the applicable tax law and explained what fraud meant to Theresa's prospects for staying out of jail and, by unspoken implication, maintaining custody of her children. I couldn't be sure, but by the end of that grim litany, I thought I saw the first faint traces of comprehension beginning to dawn in her dark eyes.

She leaned forward on the table, her coffee long forgotten. "Listen," she said. "You've got to understand. I did what he told me. That's all." She leaned back with a deep sigh. "That's all I ever did." As her understanding of the predicament she faced grew, so too did an appreciation of where her choices lay. "I got kids," she said after a long silence. "I got to make sure nothing happens to them."

"That's the most important thing," I agreed. "Your kids."

"You got to understand," she repeated, to no one in particular. "I can't go to jail. There's no one to look after them."

I stood up, my instinct telling me that we had pushed her as far as we could for the moment. We needed to give her time to think things over, to weigh her odds and consider the choices she would eventually have to make. It seemed clear that the cocky attitude she had initially confronted us with was starting to crumble. There was a distinct possibility that she would soon have to face the consequences of the crimes she had willingly, even eagerly, committed. We needed to step back and let that reality sink in.

"You think about it," I said, standing up with the others. "We'll be in touch." I told her, trying not to make it sound like a threat.

But, of course, that's what it was: a threat to the whole way of life she had chosen for herself. As we drove out of the coffee-shop parking lot, I couldn't help but wonder what her next choice would be. In my experience people don't change. Not really. After all, for twenty years Theresa Swann had done Suge Knight's bidding, vying for his affection. It's all she knew and I had my doubts, even with the custody of her children at stake, whether she could turn that corner, break free and take the second chance we were offering.

A few weeks later we had a second meeting at another Starbucks, this time in Pasadena. It was just Daryn, Bennett and me for this round, and it was my turn to do the talking. "Listen, Theresa," I said after she had sullenly turned down my offer to buy her a coffee. "We know you're in a jam. We understand what you're up against. But let me ask you something. You've lived a life of secrets and lies for so long. Don't you think it might be better now, just to let it all go?"

She nodded, her eyes cast downward, but it was hard to tell if my words had gotten through or if she was just playing along, looking to exploit any advantage presented by a softhearted cop.

"Theresa," Daryn said, the reasoned tone of his voice matching my own. "Do you know why we're here? Why we're *really* here?"

She looked up at him sharply.

"We're homicide detectives," I told her. "We want to know who killed Biggie Smalls."

Her eyes welled up. She began to cry, as far as we could tell, utterly sincere tears. It was pitiful but it was equally unavoidable. Theresa had brought herself to this moment. The truth had caught up with her. "Can you tell us what we want to know?" I asked, keeping my voice as neutral as the wood paneling around us.

She didn't answer. Other customers were starting to look over at this woman struggling to control her sobbing. A few slow seconds ticked by. I nudged Daryn and this time we both pushed back from the table, leaving Theresa alone with Bennett. "Maybe you need a few minutes to talk it over with Jeff," I said. "We'll be waiting."

The finality of the moment seemed a little unreal to both of us. Without saying a word, Daryn and I had reached the same conclusion: Theresa was our last shot at solving the case. We could keep trying, of course, keeping digging through the files, keep looking for someone who could tell us something new. But the truth was we had played our hand. There was nothing left for us to do now but wait and see how Theresa played hers.

It didn't take long before Jeff Bennett emerged through the coffee shop door, a smile on his face.

"She knows," he told us.

CHAPTER 23

The Shooter

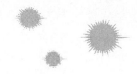

FROM THE EXPRESSION on the FBI agent's face when he announced the news, I think he expected high-fives all around. But it was way too early to celebrate. Theresa might have information about who killed Biggie Smalls and why, but this wasn't the time or place for her to tell the story. Now that we had come this far, the next step was to make it official.

A coffee shop was no place for full disclosure. I wanted to give her a chance to decompress and reflect, soberly and at length, on her available choices. I found myself hoping that she really *had* taken my words to heart, that the lying and deception would finally be over for her own good and the good of her children. Of course I'd been trying to coax her into cooperating with us, but I also believed what I'd told her, that she would have a second chance if she came clean, completely and finally.

But that had to be done in a formal setting, according to regulations, the whole nine yards in the full light of day. With Jeff still standing by to provide comfort and support, we arranged for a third meeting, this one to take place at the task force headquarters. We had reason to hope that it might well be the culmination of three years of concerted effort on the part of a team of dedicated law enforcement officers determined to bring a killer or killers to justice. Whatever our individual strengths and shortcomings had been—and there were plenty on both counts—the core of the task force was now a smoothly functioning team. We'd become adept at uncovering leads and following them as far as they could take us, even when, as in the case of Stutterbox, they had led us straight down a rabbit hole. We all had reason to be proud of the work we had done, which made it that much more imperative to bring the case home.

According to police lore, echoed in a thousand movies and TV shows, trained professionals are not supposed to get personally involved in their cases. But, of course, we often do. So it was with the task force. There was a fine line of emotional investment that some of us had crossed a long time ago. We each had our own stake in successfully concluding this investigation. For me, it was a point of pride, a matter of professional integrity. But it also stemmed from a stubborn desire to bring some measure of peace to those who still grieved the victims' violent deaths. Voletta Wallace deserved to know who had murdered her son. So did Afeni Shakur. We were determined to help bring closure to the mothers of these murdered men.

But, despite the major break we had gotten with Theresa's tentative agreement to cooperate, neither Daryn nor I were really sure we could provide those answers. We'd both seen too many interviews with witnesses go off the rails, either because the subject still had something to hide or because we'd come in with unrealistic expectations. At this critical juncture in the case, we couldn't afford to coast by simply assuming that Theresa Swann was going to deliver the killer on a platter. Above all, we had to stay on top of the process as it moved forward. There were a lot of ways the investigation could still go wrong.

It was for that reason that Daryn and I kept checking and rechecking the facts of the case to see if there was something we had, even at that point, overlooked. Our primary intent was to stay ahead of the curve, dumping as much data into our brains as they would hold before we talked to Theresa again. To the degree possible, we wanted to be able to *anticipate* what she was going to tell us. We compiled a list of those who we considered to be the most likely suspects in the Wallace murder from across the broad range of the case. And there was one name that kept reoccurring in a number of important contexts and significant circumstances: Wardell "Poochie" Fouse.

A longtime Leuder's Park Piru member, Fouse had been one of the early targets of retribution in the gang war that erupted following the killing of Tupac. He had narrowly escaped death in 2000, when he was attacked by a Crip hit squad. He wasn't so lucky when, three years later, he was shot ten times in the back while riding his motorcycle down a Compton street. Since then, Poochie had become larger in death than he had ever been in life, at least in our case files. He had been identified early on in the FBI and ATF investigation as a frequent enforcer for Suge Knight, suspected of either personally perpetrating a number of homicides or directing others to do the killing.

One telling example came to our attention through a 1997 federal task force interview with a Blood named Anthony Welch. If nothing else, his story pointed out in no uncertain terms the power that Suge Knight wielded at the juncture of rap music and gang life. Welch had recounted to the FBI the fate of William "Rat" Ratcliffe, an aspiring rapper and a member of the Bounty Hunters crew out of the Nickerson Gardens housing project in Watts. He had been pestering Suge over several months for a recording contract with Death Row Records. At one point, accompanied by ten Bounty Hunters, he had even cornered Knight in a bathroom during a video shoot, demanding to be signed.

Suge had a low tolerance for harassment, telling anyone who would listen that Rat's days were numbered. True to his word, Suge called in his trusted enforcer. According to Welch, Poochie turned up at a recording studio where Suge was producing a session, and received his marching order: get Rat. A day later Ratcliffe was run to ground on Central Avenue in Compton and summarily executed. When he heard the news, Suge reportedly commented, referring to Poochie, "He doesn't fuck around. That's how I want him to do it."

Of course, considering the company Poochie kept, the capacity to "do it" would hardly have been a distinguishing characteristic. But in contrast with the regular run of Suge's associates, what made Fouse a person of considerable interest to us was the mention of his name in a series of jailhouse letters dating back to 2004, written by a Fruit Town Piru named Roderick Reed, who was serving time on multiple drug and weapons counts. Reed had struck up a correspondence with none other than Kevin Hackie, the former Compton school officer who had played a part in Russell Poole's investigation, and would later turn up impersonating an FBI agent in the hospital waiting room where Tupac Shakur lay dying.

Apparently under the impression that Hackie could somehow be of help to him in an ongoing appeal, Reed's rambling, handwritten correspondence covered a wide range of seemingly random subjects. More often than not, however, he focused on his close connection to a Death Row Records insider who was also serving time for his role as a partner in Reed's PCP business. Letters that under other circumstances might have been dismissed as the semiliterate attempts of a convict to gain an ally on the outside, were given considerably more weight by Daryn and I, due to his links with the Death Row head. There was at least a chance that Reed actually knew what he was writing about.

And he certainly wasn't shy about sharing it. In a sequence of letters to Hackie over the summer, Reed repeatedly referred to "Poochie" Fouse as the hit man Suge Knight had used to kill Christopher Wallace in direct retaliation for the shooting of Tupac. "I no about Poochie murder Biggie Smalls," he wrote in a letter postmarked in late August, while in another, a month later, he worried that he might "dis a pear because I no Poochie murdered Biggie Smalls."

Naturally there was no way to prove Reed's allegations. At the time the letters first came to our attention, we had tried to go straight to the source. But the U.S. attorney on the case wanted Reed's scheduled appeal to run its course. The logic was that we might subsequently need to sign him on as an informant in exchange for sentencing considerations. As a result, we could do little more than file his letters away in hopes that they might come in handy when and if more evidence against Poochie emerged. It was in early May 2009, shortly before our second meeting with Theresa Swann, that just such evidence, circumstantial as it was, *did* turn up, and from a source that could be considered substantially more credible than Roderick Reed.

In the tortuous saga of the Biggie and Tupac investigations, Reginald Wright, Jr., has consistently been maligned. The former Compton police officer had founded Wright Way Protection Services, with funding from Suge Knight, as a firm whose primary clients were the artists and executives of Death Row Records. Within three weeks of Biggie's death, Wright had been named by an informant as part of a hit squad hired by Suge to carry out the killing. He had been under a cloud of suspicion ever since, despite the allegations being conclusively proven false.

In point of fact Reggie Wright, Jr., had proved a valuable resource to law enforcement, providing important information on the inner workings of Death Row and honestly concerned with the violence and greed that had overtaken the once-promising record company. It was for that reason, in the run-up to our interview with Theresa Swann, that we were interested in gaining Wright's perspective firsthand.

Agreeable and intelligent, Wright would help to lock in some of the final pieces of the puzzle Daryn and I were trying to assemble. We met with him in our offices on May 5 and immediately got to the point: what could he tell us about the murder of Biggie Smalls? While insisting that he had only heard the same rumors and speculation as everyone else, he did recall an unusual incident that had occurred shortly before the Wallace killing. Suge's brother-in-law Norris Anderson had contacted Wright about the possibility of quickly obtaining $25,000 for use in obtaining a secured credit card in the name of Theresa Swann. Norris, Wright told us, was unwilling to withdraw funds for that purpose from the Death Row accounts for fear of raising the suspicions of federal authorities who were, even then, looking into the label's financial transactions.

Wright suggested instead that Norris contact Sharitha Knight, Suge's wife. Since her husband's incarceration, Sharitha had built a successful concert promotion business under the banner of Knightlife Entertainment. She had recently returned home from managing a nationwide tour for Snoop Dogg, the superstar rapper who at that time was still on Death Row Records having just released *Tha Doggfather*, his last album for the label. Tours usually generated lots of cash, Reggie told Norris. Perhaps Sharitha could come up with the money on such short notice. As to whether Anderson ever acted on his advice, Reggie couldn't say.

"What did Theresa need all the money for?" I pressed Reggie.

He shrugged. "You'd have to ask her that," he replied laconically.

"Reggie," Daryn interjected, "was Theresa involved in the murder?"

As Wright leaned back in his chair, his expression and body language seemed to be sending a message in sharp contrast to his guarded answer.

"I don't know. Like I said, ask her."

We had every intention of doing just that, but before we let Reggie go we had one more question. Flipping through pages of reports containing information we had gathered on Suge's associates, Daryn commented on how seldom Poochie's name appeared in accounts of meetings and parties attended by Death Row principals.

"Why is that, Reggie?" he asked.

Wright again fixed us with an appraising stare. He knew what we wanted to know and we knew that he knew. But it wasn't going to go much further than that. "I can tell you this," Reggie said at last. "Suge and Poochie. That was different from everyone else. Poochie didn't hang out much. He stayed in the background. And when he did show up, it wasn't for partying. He and Suge would go off together by themselves and talk. Those two had secrets between them." He paused before adding, "And then there was the Impala."

"The Impala?' I echoed, my heart skipping a beat.

"Yeah," Reggie replied. "Poochie did some favor for Suge and Suge took him down to George Chevrolet out there on Lakewood Boulevard. Told him to pick out any car on the lot. Poochie chose an Impala."

"Was it black?" I asked, trying to keep my voice steady.

Reggie shrugged again. "I don't know," he replied. "All I know is that Suge liked it so much he bought one for himself. I guess you could say they were tight like that."

Daryn and I sat together in the empty office for a long while after Reggie had gone. We were both thinking the same thing, a process of elimination that had brought us to a conclusion that we couldn't confirm but that still seemed to us all-but inescapable.

"It was Poochie, wasn't it?" Daryn ventured at last.

I nodded: Roderick Reed's scrawled prison letters; Reggie Wright, Jr.'s enigmatic but strangely interconnected stories. None of that was particularly conclusive, not even particularly convincing. And by the same token, Poochie was just one of many hardcore gangbangers who had proven themselves capable of committing the crime. But Poochie's special relationship with Suge Knight was a compelling consideration, along with the fact that he had seemingly done just this kind of work for Suge in the past. Did that mean he was the one we'd been after all this time? Maybe we were just jumping to conclusions based on mere hints and vague suggestions. Maybe we had talked ourselves into believing we had really found the shooter.

But there we were in spite of ourselves, grappling to make sense of what we somehow suspected was the truth. A lot has been made of the special instincts required to be a cop, the celebrated "gut feeling" that operates in the realm of guesswork and conjecture. And it's true that there's often a voice in the back of your head whispering to you that things either don't add up or that they do. But police work is about more than playing your hunches. It's about certainty, empirical evidence, and a lot of times whatever certainty you may feel in your gut doesn't come with the facts to back it up. Many a case has been won and lost in the space between what you're sure of and what you can verify.

We felt sure, suddenly and completely, that Wardell "Poochie" Fouse had shot Christopher Wallace from the driver's seat of a black Chevrolet Impala outside the Petersen Automotive Museum on March 9, 1997. What we needed to do now was to prove it.

There was a lot riding on the faith we had in our own conclusions. If we were sure—really sure—then we were obliged to act, put some clout behind our conviction or call it a day. Any instinct is only as good as your willingness to follow it through. It all came down to Theresa Swann and what she might tell us at the upcoming meeting. We both had our doubts that, when it came down to it, she would be willing to come clean and tell us everything she knew. Like I said, people don't change and both Daryn and I had the sneaking suspicion Theresa would balk. She and Suge simply had too much history together, too many entangling emotional ties. We needed to find a way to make it all right for her to tell us what she might know.

CHAPTER 24

The Ruse

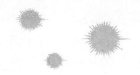

A S THE DAYS TICKED DOWN to our fateful encounter with Theresa, we became convinced that the only way to gain her full cooperation would be to try and figure out up front what she was going to tell us. We felt certain that she'd be considerably more comfortable confirming information that we already had then having to come up with it herself.

Of course, such a strategy carried with it an enormous risk. If we prompted her with our own assumptions, there would be nothing to stop her from simply agreeing with us in the hopes that we would walk away satisfied. But it wasn't going to be that simple. If she only told us what she thought we wanted to hear, we'd find out soon enough and be back, knocking at her door. Our hope was that we had provided enough incentive for her to tell us the truth. We had reasons, some substantive and some mere supposition, to believe that Poochie was the shooter. If Theresa confirmed that suspicion, we would at least have an avenue to move forward with the investigation. If not, we'd be out of options. We held our breath and gave it a shot.

We devised a ruse, as simple as it was risky. It involved putting together a sheaf of documents to present to Theresa, beginning with a driver's license Poochie had taken out under the alias of Darnell Bolton, but with a photo Swann would know to be him. We'd use it strictly for purposes of identification, making sure Theresa had no doubt about the individual we were interested in. Our next step was to create a statement we titled "*The Declaration of Darnell Bolton*," still using the name that appeared on the driver's license. This "*Declaration*" was nothing more or less than a fictitious confession put into Poochie's mouth. It consisted of fourteen numbered statements, duly witnessed and notarized by invented individuals and then signed by me, in a passable copy of Poochie's handwriting.

I, Darnell Bolton, it began, *do hereby declare and state:*

1) *I am a member of a criminal street gang known as the Mob Piru.*
2) *I am associated with members of Death Row Records, many of whom are also members of the Mob Piru gang.*
3) *I am associated with the founder and CEO of Death Row Records, namely Marion "Suge" Knight.*
4) *In the winter of 1996 and the spring of 1997, I met with Knight on various occasions to discuss Knight's desire and intention to murder Christopher "Biggie Smalls" Wallace. I understood the motive for the murder was retaliation for the murder of Tupac Shakur during the fall of 1996. Knight believed Bad Boy Records CEO Sean "Puffy" Combs had solicited the murder of Shakur, utilizing Southside Crip gang members to accomplish the killing.*
5) *I agreed to carry out the retaliation murder of Wallace in exchange for an unspecified amount of currency.*

It was here that we got even more creative. In order to make the document appear authentic we had blacked out certain portions, as if we were trying to protect sensitive information and identities, while at the same time making sure we implicated Theresa. The next item read:

6)   *I conspired with other associates of Knight's to carry out the murder, including* (redacted), (redacted), (redacted) *and Theresa Swann.*

Aside from looking great on the page, the deletions effectively disguised the fact that there were key elements to the case that we didn't yet know or were just plain making up. We continued to sprinkle blackouts through the rest of the bogus declaration.

7)   *On March 9, 1997, I arrived at the Petersen Automotive Museum and received information from* (redacted) *regarding the location of Wallace.*
8)   *I responded to that location driving a* (redacted) *in color.*
9)   *I was the sole occupant of the vehicle.*
10) *I was attired in a* (redacted) *which I discarded after the incident.*
11) (redacted) *carrying Wallace and began shooting toward him.*
12) *I left the location and discarded the gun at* (redacted). *I never saw the gun again.*
13) *I received* (redacted) *from Knight for my participation in the murder. I received such* (redacted) *female confidante Theresa Swann. I also received* (redacted) *from* (redacted).
14) *I swear the foregoing is true and correct under penalty of perjury.*

We dated it 4/1/98. April Fool's Day.

Once we had completed the dead man's declaration, we also fabricated a letter from the fictional legal firm of Manuel Quan and

Phillip Wiggins. Addressed to Chief Bratton, under the heading "*Re: Murder Investigation of Christopher Wallace Case No. 9707-19963*," the correspondence was full of bewildering legalese designed to impress Theresa with its sheer officialness. "It is our full intention," we wrote at one point, "to relinquish the written and oral declaration of the decedent for purposes of providing exculpatory evidence to be utilized and evaluated by the Court should charges in the case be brought against those believed by us to be innocent." What it meant was anybody's guess, but it looked completely legit on the fake letterhead we had invented for the occasion.

The subterfuge was complete, but whether or not it would work was a question that kept me up nights before our May 28 interview with Theresa. Maybe she'd buy the whole thing and confirm our theory that Poochie had killed Biggie Smalls. Or maybe she'd spot our scheme a mile off, throw our faked papers and our unsubstantiated conclusions back in our faces and laugh out loud. We could possibly outsmart her. Or we'd just possibly outsmart ourselves. Either way, there was no turning back. We were committed to seeing our plan through, whatever the outcome.

It was 1:30 in the afternoon when Daryn, Jeff Bennett and I finally sat down at a conference table in a spacious meeting room adjacent to the task force offices. I had chosen the locale with care: the large and roomy space was intended to calm Theresa's nerves while at the same time projecting all the power and authority that came with being on our own turf. But it was immediately clear that whatever combination of comfort and clout we presented, Theresa was already on the ragged edge. As she took a seat across from us, she immediately began to cry again, nodding mutely when we asked her to confirm for the record that the interview was voluntary.

She pulled herself together when we questioned her about legal representation, telling us that she had, in fact, consulted a lawyer, adding with a well-rehearsed line that she declined to be represented by counsel at this time. She was, it seemed, going to take her chances by facing us down on her own.

"Let's get started, then," I suggested in my most evenhanded tone.

"Look," she said. "If Suge finds out about this…" Her words trailed off. Even before we started we had reached the crux of the dilemma that Theresa had put herself in. She had to know as well as we did that there was no way we could guarantee that what she might tell us would remain confidential. Nor could we promise her that Suge would never find out about her cooperation with us. There was, first and foremost, the possibility that she might have to testify—before a grand jury or in the glaring public forum of a high profile trial—if we ever tried to advance a case against Knight based, wholly or in part, on evidence she might provide.

But the possibility of exposure went beyond even that scenario. We were cops. She was a criminal. We all knew how thin and permeable the barrier was that separated what we knew from what she knew. In a case the scope and size of the Biggie Smalls murder investigation, information has a way of leaching through either side of that barrier. Detectives often aren't privy to what another colleague has told a source, or heard from an informant. Neither can one bad guy ever be sure what a partner in crime has revealed to the police. Whatever Theresa might say to us would, it seemed likely, become part of other investigations looking into Suge's multifarious activities. All of us in that room had been around the block too many times to take bland assurances of confidentiality at face value. Making such promises might only have convinced Theresa that we were willing to say anything to gain her cooperation.

There was another transparent ploy that we also seemed, by silent consent, to quickly dispense with. Even if Theresa revealed information that resulted in a prosecution of Suge Knight, squirreling her away in a Witness Protection Program would be hugely complicated by the mere fact that she was the mother of his child. Would her right for protection trump his rights as a parent? That would seem to be the very definition of a quintessential legal quagmire.

At the same time, Daryn and I harbored the hope that the ruse we devised might provide some plausible deniability if she were ever confronted by Suge about her cooperation with us. If she believed *The Declaration of Darnell Bolton*, then she would also believe that it had been Poochie who had dropped the dime on Suge, not her. The point of our deception was to allow her to confirm what she thought we already knew, compelled to do so under the pressure of having her children, including Suge's own daughter, taken away. Under those circumstances she could probably make a very convincing case.

Of course, it was all speculation on our part. Whatever other assumptions we all shared that morning, the most obvious was our common inability to peer into the darkest recesses of Suge Knight's mind. Not even she knew what went on in there. And it was on that unknowable pivot that her choices, and ours, were balanced. Under other circumstances, protecting Theresa Swann from her complicity in the crimes of Suge Knight might have been a priority for us. But other concerns took precedence. It was clear that the choice we had presented to Theresa was agonizing. But it was certainly no more agonizing than the pain felt by Voletta Wallace over the death of her son. There were no legal ethicists assembled in that room at the crucial juncture. It was up to us to make the call as to how justice would best be served. We did the best we could.

"Theresa," Bennett replied leaning across the table. "You know we'll do our best to handle the situation."

"How you going to handle Suge?" Theresa snapped back scornfully. She stared at us in defiance, waiting for answers she knew we didn't have.

A long silence followed before Daryn took our package of bogus documents from his briefcase and pushed it across the table to Theresa.

She stared at it as if he had pulled out a rattlesnake and placed it on the table. I watched carefully as she studied Poochie's picture on the driver's license, then carefully read "*The Declaration of Darnell Bolton*" and the sham lawyer's letter. It wasn't as if I could actually see her attitude change as she studied our handiwork, but by the time she was finished some of the electric tension in the room had dissipated.

"That's right," she said, in a voice barely above a whisper. "What Poochie says, that's what happened."

I resisted the urge to look over at Daryn, not wanting my elation to give away the game. Had our strategy actually worked? Was she telling us that we had correctly identified Biggie Smalls's killer? Was the "*Declaration*" an essentially accurate account of the motivations behind the murder—in retaliation for the shooting of Tupac—not to mention the sequence of events that led to it: the contract, the payoff…all of it? I took a deep breath. Theresa *seemed* to be confirming what we suspected. But we needed to hear it from her, directly.

"Why don't you tell us what happened, Theresa?" I said. "In your own words."

At that moment, it was hard to know whether the chance we had taken by pointing her toward Poochie had really paid off. There was, instead, the ever-present possibility that we had simply provided her with a way to tell us what she thought we wanted to hear. And it was true, as she began her account, that the relief in her voice was palpable. Maybe that was because we'd given her a way to hide the truth. But it seemed just as likely that we might have provided her a way to *tell* the truth. And as her story unfolded, in a rush of details, it was hard for her to stop. She couldn't get it off her chest fast enough.

"After Tupac was shot," her account began, "Suge was real upset. I never saw him like that before, like he'd lost a brother or something. And being in jail and all, for violating his parole, that didn't help none."

"You went to see him a lot in jail," Daryn reminded her.

"All the time," Theresa nodded. "He *needed* me there. But it was hard. I had to pretend to be Kenner's assistant so they'd let me be alone with him."

"David Kenner, Suge's attorney?" I asked, wanting to get it on the record.

I knew who David Kenner was. In my line of work it would be hard *not* to know. Described by the *L.A. Times* as "a very aggressive, well-prepared criminal defense lawyer who establishes strong rapport with his clients," his name had appeared often in the course of our investigation.

Underscoring his "strong rapport," for example, was a 1996 FBI report, citing "a relationship between Suge Knight and Kenner that goes well beyond an attorney client relationship," and that included Kenner's presence "during incidents involving assaults and intimidation carried out by Knight on various victims."

Now he had turned up again, at least according to Theresa. "I come up there all dressed up like Kenner's legal secretary," she continued, "supposed to be consulting on his case. And we'd be in this room with no guards, just me and Suge and him. And most times, David wasn't paying no attention to what was going on, anyway."

"What *was* going on, Theresa?" I asked, trying to keep the narrative moving in the right direction.

The words that had been coming in a flood abruptly stopped. She looked at us looking at her, as we looked back.

"Suge said he wanted me to talk to Poochie," she continued, her voice barely audible. "You know…about Biggie."

"What about Biggie?" Daryn urged. We still needed to hear it from her.

"You know…pay Poochie to take care of him," she asserted. "'Cause of Tupac and all. He was really mad about that. Like I never saw him before. He told me where Biggie would be…you know, that party at the car museum. He told me to tell Poochie to get over there and take care of it, you know what I mean?"

"Did you?" I asked.

She nodded again. "We met a couple times," she claimed. "To talk things over."

"Where?" Daryn asked.

"That Denny's on Lakewood."

We knew the place she was talking about. It wasn't far from the Chevrolet dealership where Suge had bought Poochie a brand-new Impala in happier days. In fact, Theresa went on, Poochie had arrived at a meeting shortly after the Biggie shooting in an Impala that looked to her as if it had recently been repainted.

"What did you talk about?" Daryn and I were trading questions now, a well-oiled interrogation unit.

"About the money, mostly," she maintained. "How I could get it to him. I went back to Suge and he told me that would be all right, that he'd have it in my bank when I needed it. You know…after the thing."

I flashed back on Reggie Wright, Jr.'s account of the search for $25,000 to secure a credit card. Had that been the way the contract killing was funded?

"What happened then?" Daryn pressed.

Once again, Theresa's voice faltered. "I was there, that night, at the party," she continued after a moment. "But I left before anything happened. I swear."

"Did you see Poochie there?" I asked.

She shook her head vehemently. "I didn't see him for another couple weeks. Then he comes by, says he wants to get paid. So I go back to Suge and tell him. He put the money in the bank, just like he said."

"How much?" Daryn wanted to know.

"Nine thousand dollars, the first time."

"The first time?" I repeated.

"Poochie came back after that. Said he needed more. That he had to get out of town for a while until things cooled down. So Suge got me another four thousand. That was the last I heard of him."

A long silence followed, and in its wake Theresa began sobbing, a full-throated wail. "You can't make me say nothing in court," she cried. "I got my rights. I know my rights."

"We can't make you do anything you don't want to do," I assured her. "But we can't help you unless you help us."

"What do you think I been doing?" she demanded indignantly.

"Theresa," Daryn said, turning to face her. "How would you feel about being a documented confidential source for this investigation?"

"What's that mean?" she asked, her eyes sparking with suspicion.

"It means we want you to go to Suge," I told her. "Get him to talk."

"Talk about *what?*" There was a rising edge of hysteria in her voice.

"What you just told us. Poochie, the money, the whole thing."

Her face went slack, and she looked suddenly gaunt, hollowed out, with only her eyes alive and blazing with fear and defiance. Nothing she had told us, even between the lines, had suggested the slightest understanding of what she had done to facilitate the death of another human being. Instead, in the place of remorse, was only the primal urge for self-preservation. I felt certain that we had taken her as far as she would go. To continue would have required courage and a conscience that were simply beyond her. I understood that. I accepted it. After so many years doing what I do, you learn to take people as you find them.

Regardless, we never actually had any intention of coaxing Theresa to confirm her story by wearing a body wire and recording an incriminating conversation with Suge. Unlike Keffe D, Theresa was never going to be comfortable standing face to face with her co-conspirator and act natural while prompting him to discuss the details of the Biggie murder. From what I had seen, her body language and quivering voice would alert Suge's sixth sense and he would be frisking her for the device before the show ever started. Besides, we had something else in mind all along: a telephone wiretap.

There are strict legal conditions that must be met before a judge will grant a wiretap request. One of the primary stipulations is that all other means of investigation have been exhausted. Both Daryn and I knew beforehand that Theresa would be reluctant to wearing a recording device. But we had to go through the motions of asking her before we could approach a judge to grant us what we really wanted: to bug Suge's phone.

Of course, Theresa didn't know any of this and we wanted to keep it that way, at least until we secured the judicial go-ahead for the phone tap. The prospect of being a fly on the wall in the day-to day-life of Suge Knight had the potential to pay huge dividends in our investigation.

CHAPTER 25

Reckless Disregard

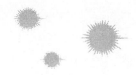

BY EARLY JUNE OF 2009, everything was falling into place. We had Keffe D ready and waiting to resume his contact with Zip Martin, who we had strong reason to believe was the supplier of the weapon used to kill Tupac Shakur. If we could get Zip on tape acknowledging that fact, it would go a long way toward confirming Keffe D's account of the murder and the rest of the case might then fall into place. At the same time, I had started working on a wiretap request for Suge's phone, in the hope that we could convince Theresa Swann to make the calls that would elicit information confirming our theory that Poochie had murdered Biggie Smalls at Suge's behest. Everything was set to go.

As a troubled kid, my adoptive dad, a Pop Warner football coach, had taught me the value of a good sports metaphor, and it was only natural for me to see the results of our team's hard work in football terminology. I was the task force quarterback and Daryn Dupree was my running back. It was the fourth quarter of the championship playoff and the two-minute warning had just sounded in a game that had seen us relentlessly drive the ball all the way to the one-yard line. Our efforts had been so outstanding that we'd even gotten some of the opposing team to play for us. One final, concerted effort to get over the goal line was all it would take to score the winning touchdown.

But an unforeseen and unwelcome circumstance arose that made it extremely difficult to keep my eye on the ball for that last crucial play. The disruption harkened back to the George Torres investigation I had worked off and on from 1997 up to the time I joined the task force eight years later. As part of the Torres investigative team, I had focused on building a criminal case against the grocery store magnate, culminating on raids of nine Numero Uno markets. There we had gathered evidence pointing to the intimidation of shoplifters through extortion and false imprisonment. I had developed evidence of Torres' involvement in a number of homicides. The investigation had more or less been wrapped up by the time I joined the revived Wallace investigation.

Nearly sixty counts against Torres had been handed down by a grand jury in February 2005. From that point on, the case took a protracted and convoluted course through the courts. Assistant U.S. Attorney Tim Searight, handling a RICO prosecution for the first time, worked hard to get the trial heard before a U.S District Court judge who had a reputation for being "pro-government." Unfortunately, Searight hadn't taken into consideration the judge's attitude toward all-encompassing RICO prosecutions, which he seemed to feel were examples of unwarranted federal overreach. During pretrial hearings he let it be known that he didn't care for the "architecture" of the government's case and went on to comment that the individual RICO charges against Torres should have been handled separately in lower state courts. The prospects for the prosecution were further called into question by another remark the judge made from the bench. "Let's face it," he said, "this case is going to be tried on murder. No one is going to jail forever for cheating on their taxes or hiring illegal immigrants. It's all about these murders, so let's get it on."

With those words he effectively narrowed the scope of the prosecution to the three murders I had investigated. The head of Torres's defense team took note and immediately adjusted their trial strategy, relentlessly focusing on discrediting the homicide charges. Which meant discrediting me.

At the same time, the defense filed a motion to suppress the evidence that we had gathered from the grocery store raids, claiming that probable cause existed for the search of only one store and not all nine. The judge ruled in their favor, basing his decision on what he considered inaccurate statements that I had made on the search warrant request. The disputed passages were taken from wiretap conversations I had monitored and interviews I had conducted with various Torres associates. When writing the affidavit for the search warrant I had, in the words of a subsequent inquiry, "paraphrased the interview... drawing from the conversation as a whole, rather than from a literal dictation."

On such small pivots whole cases and years of work can stand and fall. In his supporting statement on the motion to suppress, the judge asserted that I had made "inaccurate statements intentionally or with reckless disregard for the truth." A verbatim account of my interview, he continued, would have "negatively affected the magistrate's finding of probable cause" in determining the scope of the search.

Spurred by the finding on their behalf, the defense team launched an all-out attack. If I had lied on the search warrant affidavit, what else was I lying about? I was, they claimed, obsessed with George Torres and would do anything to see him put away, including threatening and bribing witnesses. The thrust of the defense's strategy as it played out in the media was succinctly summed up in the headline of a local paper: *"Detective Greg Kading Was Fixated On George Torres. Did He Go Too Far?"*

There is a lot I could say in my own defense. I could point out the daunting complexity of writing a search warrant request that balances the stringent standards for probable cause with the often-urgent requirements of an ongoing investigation. I could insist that the minor misquotations in my affidavit had no substantive impact on the case. But I'm not going to. What I will say is that I made a mistake. I got careless in drafting a document I had written a hundred times before. In doing so, I left myself vulnerable to an attack by Torres's attorneys and they took full advantage of the opening I had unwittingly provided.

Despite the setback, I was still confident of a favorable outcome in the upcoming trial. That assurance was bolstered by the fact that Searight and his team seemed undeterred by the ruling. The evidence that was thrown out had to do only with the extortion charges. There were still close to sixty counts left on the indictment, ranging from fraud to money laundering to tax evasion. Also still on the docket were the homicides I had investigated. The trial finally got under way, on March 24, just at the point when we were beginning to get traction with Theresa Swann.

From its opening statement the defense team tried to make the case about me. What was less clear was Searight's plan for countering the attack. Despite my repeated requests that he put me on the stand, the U.S. Attorney continued to insist that we wait until the defense called me. "Every case needs a boogie man," he told me. "Let's wait until they try to prove what they're saying against you. Then we'll make our move."

The problem was the defense never intended to have me testify. It was, in fact, imperative to keep me *off* the stand, where I could refute their allegations and defend myself. As a result, the assertions of Torres's defense team were allowed to go unanswered. After almost a month, the defense rested without having called me. Yet, for all of their legal skill they had failed to convince the jury. On April 20, guilty verdicts on fifty-eight of the fifty-nine counts against Torres, including one of the three murder charges, were handed down. I took each of them as a personal vindication, regardless of the damage that my reputation had sustained. Despite the missteps, Searight had pulled off what appeared to be a major legal victory. We all had reason to feel good about the outcome of our protracted efforts to bring a prosecution against George Torres.

That feeling didn't last long. Within three weeks of the verdict being read, the defense was demanding the conviction be overturned on the basis on yet another legal technicality. In a 147-page decision effectively voiding the conviction, the judge ruled that procedures had been violated. After spending two years in federal custody, George Torres was a free man. In postmortems on the Torres debacle, several legal specialists, speaking on background, offered their considered opinions as to why the case had gone down in flames, some pointing to Searight directly, claiming he was intimidated by the judge's appearance of prejudice against the prosecution. Others pointed the finger squarely at the bench. According to one federal prosecutor familiar with the case, "A good defense attorney is going to sense a sympathetic judge and argue every technicality he can. Judges can't control jury deliberation, but they can control post-trial motions… (The defense) kept pushing to see how far he could go in taking the case apart and he went pretty far."

Suffice it to say, a jury of George Torres' peers had found him guilty of fifty-eight criminal counts, including solicitation of murder. His attorney nullified that judgment with a legal technicality. In the process I had become collateral damage.

CHAPTER 26

Perception

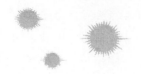

B Y MIDSUMMER OF 2009, I had effectively put the Torres fiasco behind me. But the outcome of the trial had an unexpected impact on the Biggie and Tupac investigations, even then moving forward into their final stages.

The reputation of Assistant U.S. Attorney Tim Searight, who otherwise had impeccable credentials and a near-flawless record as a federal prosecutor, was compromised by the ultimate outcome of the Torres trial, despite the fact that he made the case on its merits and that the dismissal fit the classic definition of losing on a technicality. But I was aware that the damage sustained by Searight might well bleed over into any prosecutable case that we developed against Puffy and Suge. Searight, who had provided invaluable legal oversight for the task force from the beginning, would naturally be taking those cases to trial if we could provide him with the necessary evidence. It was a difficult decision, but in the end I couldn't risk jeopardizing our chances in court with a prosecutor whose professional standing, rightly or wrongly, had been called into question. I concluded that the best course of action would be to abandon the racketeering aspects of the case and hone in on the murders themselves. After utilizing all the advantages afforded to us by coming under the federal umbrella, now, at the eleventh hour, I was forced to bring the case back under local control.

Accordingly, I reached out to an L.A. deputy district attorney to discuss the possibility of transferring the murder cases to his jurisdiction. After talking over the issue with Searight, the DA told me he had no problem with proceeding on the case himself. That difficult issue resolved, my focus then turned to completing our strategy for bringing the investigations home. I had reason to be hopeful. The task force had managed, against the longest of odds, to reopen two famous, and famously cold, cases to the verge of a successful conclusion. Considering the distance we had come, what was left to accomplish, while still formidable, was within our grasp. Nothing, it seemed, could stop us now.

Until something did.

On July 22, 2009, I arrived at work at 6:00 am as usual to begin my day. Two hours later, Lieutenant Thomas Thompson, my immediate superior, arrived to tell me that Commander Pat Gannon wanted to see me at 9:00. Naturally, I was a bit apprehensive about this sudden summons from the brass and I told Thompson as much.

"Is there a problem?" I asked. "Am I in some kind of trouble?"

"There's no problem," the lieutenant tersely responded. I took him at his word and an hour later he was back to personally escort me to Gannon's office.

I entered the large comfortable room, hung with commendations and photos of the commander posing with various VIPs. Outside the windows overlooking downtown Los Angeles, the morning was coming up bright and clear. Gannon, a seasoned veteran with a personable and understated approach that belied his rank, invited me to sit down.

"Greg," he began, immediately cutting to the chase, "I want you to know up front that this is coming straight from the chief's office. This is not my decision. You may not understand it right away, but this is being done to protect you."

"What's being done?" I asked in a low voice, my heart suddenly pounding in my chest. Thompson hadn't been straight with me: there *was* a problem. And from the tone of Gannon's voice, it was a big problem.

"As of today," he continued, "you are off the Biggie Smalls task force. You need to know that an Internal Affairs complaint has been generated. We're looking into it, but in the meantime, you're suspended from the investigation."

A stunned silence followed. There were only two times in my career that I cried. One was when a partner got shot in the line of duty. The other was in Pat Gannon's office. I wanted to shout out loud that the decision to take me off the case—a case to which I had given every-thing—made no sense. As a career LAPD officer I was accustomed to the often inscrutable policies of departmental bureaucracy. I was familiar with the sometimes queasy blend of policing and politics that resulted in decisions that the rank and file was simply forced to swallow. I had heard too many times that the reason for some irrational action was on a need-to-know basis, above our pay grade, for the good of the department or for our own good. I'd learned to accept all that as an unavoidable condition for doing the work I loved.

But this was different. I knew, as I came to believe that the LAPD also knew, that taking me off the case would stop it in its tracks. I'd seen it happen too many times. A detective, or a team of detectives, who gave their all to an investigation, get transferred or reassigned or moved along for whatever reason. Lacking the motivating force of those individuals who have pushed a case forward by dedication and sheer hard work, an investigation withers and dies, the guilty go free, and the innocent are denied justice.

It had happened with Joannie McNamara, my training officer back at Newton, when she was yanked from the original Torres case after threats were made on her life. It had happened to the FBI and ATF task force that had worked so long to build a RICO prosecution against Death Row Records, only to be reassigned in the wake of 9/11. Now it was happening to me.

Over the course of my tenure with the task force, I had taken on the role of leader, not just because I wanted it, but because I deserved it. I worked night and day on the most challenging investigation of my career. But that wasn't the only reason and not even the most important one. There were people who needed to know what had happened. It wasn't just the family and friends of Biggie and Tupac who deserved those answers. It was the public at large, the ones who paid my salary to solve crimes. I owed it to them to complete the task I'd been assigned as much as I owed it to myself to finish what I'd started.

Now, without warning, at the one-yard line in the final minute of the fourth quarter, I was being pulled from the game. I wanted to scream, to punch something, to upend Gannon's big oak desk. But instead I just stood there, vaguely aware of the commander's voice droning in the background. "I wanted to meet with you to offer you the chance to express your opinion," he was saying and for a moment my tears nearly turned to bitter laughter. What good would my opinion do? The decision had already been made and there was no doubt that it was final. I deserved to know why this was happening. I'd earned that right. But that didn't mean I was going to get it. Nothing I could say was going to prompt them to open this can of worms and let me peek inside. But, in that moment, I just couldn't help myself.

"Why?" I asked.

Gannon barely blinked. It was as if, anticipating the question, he had already rehearsed the answer. "Allegations were made in the Torres case," he told me. "We know they're baseless, Greg, totally without foundation. But there's a perception out there and we're concerned that it might work against you and the Biggie case. This is for the best. Believe me."

I knew as soon as I heard his justification that it was utterly point-less to remind him of the facts. The Torres defense team had succeeded in making the trial about me. The mistakes I had made on the search warrant were completely irrelevant to the substance of the charges against the grocery man. I had obediently toed the department line, repeatedly responding to press questioning with the obligatory "No comment." I had never been allowed to refute accusations against me due to Searight's fateful decision not to call me as a prosecution witness. But none of that mattered. There was, in Gannon's words, "a perception." For the LAPD that perception had become reality.

But even as I realized the tawdry reality of what he was saying, I knew it wasn't the whole story. The LAPD was far too experienced in having their actions and inactions tried in the court of public opinion to really take the accusations made against me all that seriously. They knew what bad press was about and had long since learned to take it in stride. I firmly believe that the reason I had been taken off the investigation had, in the end, less to do with the Torres case than with other, more cynical calculations.

On the morning I met with Commander Gannon, the Biggie Smalls investigation had remained unsolved for 4,448 days. The only reason it had been resurrected in 2006 was because of the threat of a massive judgment against the department in the civil suit brought by the Wallace family. That suit had been fueled by Russell Poole's theory implicating the police. But we had all but totally disproved that particular hypothesis, once and forever. There was no police conspiracy. There never had been and the exculpatory truth we had so painstakingly uncovered would, I'm certain, become the key to the department's subsequent deliberations.

Shortly before I was called into Gannon's office, the LAPD had received the opinion of an outside law firm retained to weigh the likely result of the civil suit should it come to trial. The conclusion: the LAPD should consider settling for $2 million, a price that would, in all probability, be far exceeded by the costs of a trial, particularly given the unpredictable nature of many civil proceedings. The LAPD, in short, was still vulnerable to what the attorneys termed "death by a thousand cuts," the slow whittling away of credibility by the family's lawyers, which could ultimately sway the jury in a city where mistrust of the police was rampant.

But the LAPD decided not to take that advice. The reason, I believe, was simple: by the diligent efforts of the task force, we had decisively undercut the rationale that had spawned the civil case in the first place. If push came to shove in court on the issue of police involvement in the murder, all they would have to do was produce the evidence we had obtained. The LAPD was effectively off the hook. And the task force had outlived its usefulness.

But what about the murderers, and the murdered? What about the long arm of the law? Of course, the alleged shooters, Baby Lane and Poochie, had long been in their graves. But what about the evidence that pointed to the involvement of others? Did it matter that those individuals were still walking free, or that the crimes we suspected they had committed would now almost certainly go unpunished?

It's my belief that the LAPD carefully weighed its options and decided that, all things considered, it best suited them to let sleeping dogs lie. It also stands to reason that there were other considerations that figured into the decision. They knew, because we had kept them up to date on our progress, that tapping Suge Knight's phone might provide the critical mass of evidence required to file charges. After that, in the midst of the inevitable media frenzy that would ensue, all bets were off. Any defense lawyer worth his exorbitant fee would resurrect the well-worn speculation of police involvement, accusing the department of railroading Suge to keep its dark secrets hidden. In all likelihood, and given the case we had built, such a strategy would have failed. But now there was a wild card in the equation that could trigger all kinds of unintended consequences.

I was that wild card. As the sole target of the defense in the Torres case, I would predictably become the poster boy for a police cover-up in any Suge Knight trial. I had already been accused of "reckless disregard" in my faulty preparation of a search warrant. It would be irresistible for any defense attorney to point out to a jury that I had authored the vast majority of documents in the Biggie case, up to and including several search warrants.

None of this occurred to me as I sat in Gannon's office that morning. I was in shock, overwhelmed by rage and sorrow and the troubling feeling that somehow I was to blame for what had just happened. Had I been, as the press painted me in the heat of the Torres trial, "overzealous"? Had I become too involved in the Biggie case, too close to the victims and the perpetrators? I had gotten to know these people on a first-name basis, trying not to be their judge and jury, to sort out their sins, but simply to do my job. Was there some invisible line I had stepped over, separating the professional from the personal? Was this payback for that indiscretion?

The rush of emotions I was feeling was more than I could handle. I needed to get away, out of that office, out of that building, and try to come to terms with what had just happened. But even then I felt a tug of responsibility. "Commander Gannon," I said, finally overcoming the quaking in my voice. "Sir, there is one thing I'd like to request."

"What is it, Greg?" he replied, and I thought I could hear a faint note of regret in his voice. Not that it mattered, but in that moment I think he understood what I was going through.

I swallowed hard. "Please make sure that whoever takes over for me on this case has the ability and experience to finish what we started."

"Of course," he said, but I didn't break the stare that was fixed between us.

"Sir," I said with all the sincerity I could muster. "I'm begging you." I turned and left without another word. The meeting had lasted ten minutes. It was the longest ten minutes of my life.

I didn't immediately tell anyone on the team what had happened. It was too soon and there were too many untethered thoughts colliding in my mind. I slipped out of the office and headed home. It was on that long stretch of freeway that I began slowly but surely to put my suspension from the task force into a larger context.

My hindsight is as perfect as the next guy's, and with 20/20 vision I was beginning to see how all this fit into the larger context of the LAPD's unspoken but ironclad policies. The department has long tended toward those actions and decisions that would ensure its own survival, even at the cost of its public responsibility. I'm not accusing the LAPD of corruption—like any other large metropolitan police force it has its share of crooked cops—but what the LAPD is guilty of is, in some ways, worse. It isn't just incompetence. It is a lack of conviction, an institutional inability to do the right thing by its officers and, more important, by those it is sworn to serve.

In some ways, I suppose, the decision to remove me could be seen as a prudent response to a difficult situation. Given the stains on the department's reputation, trying the Biggie Smalls murder case would have certainly been problematic. I understood that. It was one of the reasons I had pushed for insulating the investigation by federalizing the task force at its inception. I knew that, when the time came, the department would need to be protected against the inevitable accusations of complicity. But instead, when the time came, the department blinked. Rather than manning up to bring these killers to justice, it chose to hedge its bets, letting the investigation die an unnatural death rather than risk the potentially damaging, but ultimately insubstantial, flak that would surely come its way. It was all too easy to throw me under the bus rather than follow the investigation to its righteous outcome.

Of course, the department had a long history of overreaction to perceived threats to its existence. The Rampart Scandal of the late nineties was a prime example. Based on the allegations of Rafael Perez, a crooked cop if ever there was one, the LAPD fired, suspended, or reassigned dozens of good officers at the division. Instead of weathering a storm of public outrage over a scandal that had no merit, the department besmirched the reputations of some of its finest. It was a decision that would come back to haunt it, in the form of numerous civil suits filed by the disgraced officers, which would eventually cost the city millions of dollars in settlements and restitution.

But the brass hadn't learned from that expensive experience. It was doing the same thing all over again, this time to me. I was a decorated officer, a veteran investigator at the top of my field. But because of a "perception" I was deemed too compromised to continue leading a high-profile case.

At least that's what they told me. As I traced the ribbon of freeway out of downtown and into the open stretches of suburbia, I couldn't figure out for the life of me what was true anymore and what was a lie. I was hurting. That's all I knew.

It took me the better part of a year to get over that hurt, to finally begin to understand what happened, and to do something about it.

CHAPTER 27

Policy and Procedure

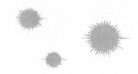

OVER THE COURSE OF that year I remained at the LAPD, even as my anger and anguish over the action that had been taken, regularly rose and fell. In the immediate aftermath of my removal from the task force, my initial impulse was to simply take my retirement. It was my friends and family who urged me to step back from my raw emotions and carefully consider my next move. They were right. I needed time to sort out my conflicts and confusion.

And one of the most conflicted and confusing issues I faced had to do with the way the department was treating me in the aftermath of its decision. Instead of regarding me as a pariah, whose reputation, as they claimed, had been indelibly stained, they told me to take my pick of any job I wanted. The offer compounded the disconnect I was feeling about the department's true motives for removing me from the task force. If I had been so fatally compromised by my involvement in the Torres case, why would they hand me any plum assignment

I asked for? Wouldn't it make more sense to stick me away in some musty desk job, out of sight and out of mind?

On reflection, it only served to underscore what I increasingly suspected, that by decapitating the task force the department hoped the case would dry up and blow away. Their purpose, plain and simple, was to pull the plug, and it had nothing to do with any perception of my integrity, or lack thereof. By providing me with this backhanded vote of confidence, they had tipped their hand as to their actual intent. Giving me any assignment I requested was their way of trying to placate me, to keep me quiet.

I had been the investigative head of what, by any reckoning, was among the most famous cold cases in American criminal history, one that was ostensibly a top priority for the LAPD. Once they pulled me off that job, they assigned me to another high-profile investigation that the department had also vowed to solve, come hell or high water. Beginning in the late eighties, a task force had been assigned to find the serial killer responsible for the deaths of eight women, their bodies found in dumpsters and alleyways in and around South Central Los Angeles. Originally dubbed the Southside Slayer, the perpetrator was renamed the Grim Sleeper by the press when he reappeared after a nearly fourteen-year hiatus. But, as important as it was to find the Grim Sleeper, I found myself unable to muster much enthusiasm for my new job. I had grown accustomed to a hands-on, proactive approach to investigative work. It was easy to see that the detectives on the Grim Sleeper task force could only wait around for a DNA hit that would match the evidence that had been gathered at the various crime scenes over the years. It wasn't my idea of police work, although in the end the investigators, all of them highly competent professionals, identified the perpetrator by the breakthrough use of familial DNA, pinpointing a match through the killer's son. It was solid, innovative forensics work that deservedly made headlines. But by that time I was already gone.

Not long into my tenure with the Grim Sleeper team, I decided that what I really missed was breaking cold cases. Tracing the faintest of trails, recovering lost evidence, reimagining the crime itself…that was a part of *my* DNA. I asked to be reassigned to the Cold Case unit and immediately stumbled across an intriguing thirty-four-year-old unsolved rape-and-murder case. The victim had been an eighty-year-old woman living in West L.A. in 1975. In the course of the sexual assault, her assailant had left his DNA traces. Thanks to the improved database that had been developed over the intervening years, we were able to match the genetic material to an itinerant laborer who had been sixteen at the time he committed the horrendous crime. It got even more horrendous after we brought him in. The suspect, who literally shit his pants during our interview, denied any involvement in the incident. Since we had a positive DNA match, his protestations of innocence were as good as a confession, and we set about to further bolster the case against him. We located a bank robber serving time in a Minnesota mental hospital who admitted to being a party to the murder by suffocation. He was, however, insistent that no rape had occurred. Putting together a timeline of the crime, we realized that our suspect had actually returned to the victim's home to have sex with her corpse.

I can't say that getting such a glimpse into real human depravity improved my attitude toward my job. But there was something about the rhythm and routine of investigative work that eventually blunted my initial determination to retire. I was doing what I'd always done, what I did best, and there was a certain satisfaction in that. But it was what remained *undone* that continued to color my outlook, despite my best efforts to move on. That outlook grew considerably darker as I saw the direction the Biggie Smalls investigation was taking in my absence. I did my best to keep tabs on the progress of the case, at the same time being careful not to put Daryn into the compromising position of revealing what was, after all, still tightly guarded information. But

I was able to stay up to date just by keeping my eyes and ears open, and what I learned only deepened my frustration and resentment over the department's handling of the case. Instead of responding to my heartfelt plea to put an effective and knowledgeable detective in charge of the task force, they had instead replaced me with someone I considered to be one of the least capable candidates: Alan Hunter.

Simply put, I had no confidence that Hunter was suited to handle an investigation with the multifaceted complexity of the Wallace probe. A by-the-book officer, he demonstrated early on his seeming lack of interest in the details of the investigation and not once after assuming control of the task force did he request a meeting with me to be debriefed. I understood and acknowledged that we had personal issues. To the degree that I bore responsibility for that animosity, I was willing to make amends and move on for the sake of the case. Hunter, for his part, apparently didn't see the necessity in reaching out to the one person who knew the most about the job he'd been assigned to complete. But, for me, the truth was now all but unavoidable. Hunter *hadn't* been assigned to finish the job. He was there for one purpose only: to shut the investigation down. It was, I became convinced, just one more element of the LAPD's strategy to bury the case once and for all with a policy of not-so-benign neglect.

Shortly after I was pulled off, the task force abruptly received instructions to hand over to the Las Vegas police all the evidence that had been gathered in the murder of Tupac Shakur. So much for our carefully considered strategy to keep LVMPD out of the loop for the time being. We had made that decision to prevent them from compromising our star informant, Keffe D. Once they had been apprised of his involvement in the Tupac murder, LVMPD could easily justify making an arrest. When that happened, of course, the case would fall apart.

It was almost as if, in some surreal way, Russell Poole had been right all along. The LAPD *was* trying to cover up the Biggie Smalls murder, not by protecting corrupt cops but by undercutting the ability of its own investigators to solve the case. What they had to hide was not culpability in the killing but rather a studied disregard for justice. It was expedient for them to cripple the case in the interests of avoiding a potentially difficult prosecution. That expediency trumped everything, including the pledge to "Protect and Serve" stenciled on the door of every black-and-white patrol car in the city.

But turning over evidence to the Las Vegas police would be only the first step in what seemed like a concerted effort to dismantle the case. What happened next goes a long way toward proving that simple, garden-variety incompetence in law enforcement can do as much damage as any conspiracy to undermine law and order. I learned from a contact in the district attorney's office that, in the waning months of 2009, Hunter made the decision to scrap the wiretap. Instead, he proposed signing Theresa on as an informant with the intent of sending her back to Suge wearing a body wire. This was wrong on so many different levels, not least of which was the fact that, as an official informant, Theresa would no longer be motivated to cooperate. And in case Hunter missed that point, Theresa's newly hired attorney proceeded to make it clear in no uncertain terms, demanding that Theresa be granted immunity from the charges she was facing in exchange for her further assistance in the case.

By this single action, Hunter undercut any incentive for Theresa to work with them. Moving forward, especially by wearing the body wire, Swann could claim that she had already done her best to gather evidence against Suge, regardless of the outcome. Any leverage the task force had over her had now been forfeited. She could simply waive her immunity flag. Theresa was working for the government now. No one was going to send her to jail. Hunter had not only initiated procedures that seemed specifically designed to undercut the considerable progress Daryn and I had made, he also failed to follow-up on our most promising leads. Theresa had identified Poochie as the shooter, but the task force never used the photo on his 1997 driver's license as part of a "6-pack" of mug shots that could have been shown to witnesses such as Eugene Deal, Lil' Cease and D-Roc Butler, who might have identified him as the man with the fade haircut behind the wheel of the black Impala that night outside the Petersen. Nor was Jewell questioned about her presence at the party and what she might have seen. More to the point, Theresa Swann was never subpoenaed to testify before a grand jury, an essential step in any projected prosecution of this nature. It was clear enough that the investigation was circling the drain.

In the meantime, I had been making persistent inquiries as to the exact nature of the Internal Affairs complaint that Commander Gannon said had been made against me. Like everything else regarding an evaluation of my involvement in the Torres case, information was being stonewalled. Nobody, it seemed, could tell me who had filed the complaint with the IA, what infraction I was supposed to have committed, or how the department intended to handle the matter. Vague references to the faulty search warrant were alluded to, but no one would or could say for sure. Patience was advised, along with a lot of shoulder shrugging and weary references to the snail's pace of bureaucracy.

But I wasn't buying it. I couldn't help but wonder if the LAPD might not be holding the ongoing IA investigation over my head as a way of silencing my objections to the fate of the task force. I have no way to prove any of this, of course, but what kept coming back to me in those days and weeks was the legal concept of Preponderance of Evidence. Maybe I didn't have enough to flat-out accuse the LAPD of hindering an ongoing investigation or intimidating one of its own detectives. What I knew for sure, what I felt in my gut, was that it all added up to something. I just didn't know what.

Then, on April 19, 2010, a federal judge abruptly dismissed the latest in a string of civil lawsuits that the Wallace family had been filing against the LAPD since 2002, alleging police involvement in the Biggie shooting. Aside from being the last gasp of Russell Poole's theory, the dismissal of the suit, without prejudice, removed the last impediment to the LAPD's plan to shelve the case. No threat of a mega million-dollar judgment remained, no chance of a "death by a thousand cuts." They were, finally and completely, off the hook. In a bitter irony, the attorney for the Wallace estate announced in public that the plaintiff, to avoid hampering what he called a "reinvigorated" police investigation, had withdrawn the suit. "The criminal investigation has been opened back up full force," he asserted. Asked by reporters about the exact state of the Biggie case, the commander of the Robbery-Homicide Division spoke in artful circles. "It's always been considered an open investigation," he said. "We've never filed a case on somebody or said we had it solved." As if to underscore the point, he added that there were *no new* suspects currently under investigation. What he neglected to mention, of course, was just how close we had come to exactly that outcome. When asked if the police were any closer to resolving the thirteen-year-old case, he snapped back, "Probably not."

The dismissal of the civil suit effectively hammered the last nail into the coffin of the investigation. Formed in direct response to the threat of a lawsuit, the task force was quickly dismantled when that threat evaporated, without regard to the fundamental question it was charged with answering: who killed Christopher Wallace and Tupac Shakur? Not that it mattered. Not anymore. Within weeks of the dismissal, it was announced that the remaining members of the team had exactly one month to finish their work, draw whatever conclusions they cared to, and call it a day. I guess one of the most painful aspects in that forlorn interlude was watching from across the room as Hunter and Dupree methodically packed away all the task force case files, piling up cardboard transfer boxes waiting to be returned to the archives.

Not long afterward, I finally received the Internal Affairs report on the complaint that had been filed against me. The substance of their findings did indeed concern the flawed search warrant request I had written during the Torres investigation. My infraction dealt with an interview I had conducted with Torres' brother Manuel regarding company practices at the grocery chain. "In transcripts of the recording," the report read, "Kading used the word 'procedure' instead of 'policy.'"

That was it: the sum and substance of the Internal Affairs investigation that the LAPD had dangled over me for a year. I didn't know whether to laugh or cry. My reputation, they had regretted to inform me, had been compromised by a perception so damaging they were forced to remove me from the task force. And this, in the end, was the best they could come up with? I had been railroaded and they hadn't even bothered to put a real locomotive on the tracks. I didn't know whether it was a tragedy or some sort of twisted comedy. But I did know one thing. My career in the Los Angeles Police Department, to which I had given twenty-two years of dedicated service, was over.

I did due diligence on the handful of cases that remained on my desk. I had my weapon and badge framed in a handsome display box. I took Daryn out to lunch and we talked and laughed about the old days, the better days. Keffe D and Zip Martin and Theresa Swann and Poochie and Stutterbox—especially Stutterbox: we acknowledged them all, good and bad, as some of the most intense and involving individuals we had ever met. In a way, it had been a privilege to know them all, worthy opponents who had given us a run for our money. And in the end they got away. There was no denying that. But we'd come close, so close, and that was something to be proud of, an accomplishment that no one could take away.

The next morning, I went downstairs to the personnel office and submitted my retirement papers.

EPILOGUE

CASES HAVE A WAY OF coming back around, even the cold ones…especially the cold ones. Years go by with no new leads. Witnesses die and evidence disappears. But, despite being buried in the sands of time, the dead still cry out for justice. I truly believe that.

I never intended to walk away from the Biggie Smalls and Tupac Shakur murder investigations. Not even when I retired from the force…especially not then. I knew I still had something to do, that there was one option left for me to bring the truth to light.

You're holding that option in your hands.

I could never have written a book about what I knew and how I knew it if I was still a cop. There's a document called the *"Law Enforcement Code of Ethics"* by which I lived my professional life. It states in part, "Whatever I see or hear of a confidential nature or that is confided to me in my official capacity will be kept ever secret unless revelation is necessary in the performance of my duty."

As long as I was wearing a badge I couldn't betray that oath. But, by the same token, what was "necessary in the performance of my duty" had remained unfinished. I needed to quit in order to persevere, to leave the force in order to fulfill my sworn duty.

I hope this book serves the purposes for which it was intended. I want it to bring closure to the families of Christopher Wallace and Tupac Shakur. I want it to reveal the truth about their deaths, a truth that has been hidden and distorted and bent to suit a dozen different agendas. I want to make it known how the case had almost been solved and who was responsible for the failure to see it through.

But more than anything, I want to keep the case *alive*. Perhaps this book will serve as a spur for the LAPD to do the right thing, to reopen the case one more time and finally conclude the investigation on the basis of the evidence it already has or is not too late to gather.

Baby Lane and Poochie are gone. But Suge Knight isn't. Neither is Zip Martin, or Theresa Swann or Terrence Brown, or several other principal players in the murders.

Of course, they could deny it all, every word I've written in these pages. They could hire lawyers to argue that the sources we used to solve the murders were unreliable criminals, the scum of the earth, acting under duress, who just happened to tell convincing, compelling, and coherent narratives.

Maybe this story would never hold up in court. But maybe it will hold up in the court of public opinion.

You decide.

ACKNOWLEDGMENTS

IN THE LAPD: Captain Kyle Jackson, Captain Denis Cremins, Lieutenant Don Hartwell, Detective Brian Tyndall, Detective William Holcomb, Detective Frank Trujilllo, and Sergeant Omar Bazulto.

In the DEA: Special Agents Briane Grey, Sean Vickers, Amin Fard, and Task Force Officers Chris Marshall and Tim Harrington.

In the FBI: Special Agents Dan McMullin, Danny Martinez, Craig Harris, Charles Gravis, and Mecole Spencer.

In the BATF: Special Agents John Ciccone and James Black.

In the IRS: Special Agent Mark Pearson.

In the LA County Sheriffs Department: Lieutenant Tracee Edmonds, Lieutenant Randy Dickey, Lieutenant Dave Coleman, Detective Karen Shonka, Detective Greg Thurman, and Detective Tim Brennan.

Special thanks to Daryn Dupree, a great detective, a great partner, and an even better friend.

To my wife, Donna, and son Dane, "I love you both beyond words".

And to those I can't publicly acknowledge, thank you for all your encouragement and support on this project.

Michele, Ronda and the team at *1106 Design* for the cover art and layout design: Thank you for your patience and professionalism.

To Glenda Ebersole at *E Grafxx* for web design and business logo: Thank you too, for all your patience and professionalism.

To my agents Paul Bresnick and Joel Gotler: Thanks for believing in this book and all your efforts to push it forward.

Thanks to Don Seitz and Marcus Chait for giving me invaluable insight and instruction on this newly traveled road.

Thanks to Tyson Cornell at *Rare Bird Lit.* for planning and execution

Thank you John and Sophia, for having my back past, present, and future.

And to Davin Seay, who brought this story to life and gave me a new friend in the process. You are a Godsend!

And speaking of God: To the King of Kings and Lord of Lords, thank You for "all things".

ABOUT THE AUTHOR

G REG KADING is a retired Los Angeles Police Department detective. Specializing in the fields of gangs, narcotics, and homicide, Detective Kading spent most of his career assigned to federal task forces to investigate complex criminal cases in the City of Angels. Decorated with the Medal of Valor for bravery and Police Star for heroic action, Detective Kading achieved the departments highest ranking as an investigator. After his 25-year law enforcement career he retired in 2010 to write this book.

Greg Kading lives in southern California with his wife, Donna, and two bulldogs, Ricky Bobby and Evil. He is the proud father of a son, Dane, who is a Marine serving in Afghanistan.

CPSIA information can be obtained at www.ICGtesting.com
Printed in the USA
BVOW040852050612

291783BV00001BA/6/P